Elizabeth Rundle Charles

Mary

The Handmaid of the Lord

Elizabeth Rundle Charles

Mary
The Handmaid of the Lord

ISBN/EAN: 9783337118365

Printed in Europe, USA, Canada, Australia, Japan

Cover: Foto ©ninafisch / pixelio.de

More available books at **www.hansebooks.com**

MARY, THE HANDMAID OF THE LORD.

By the same Author.

I.

CHRONICLES OF THE SCHONBERG-COTTA FAMILY.

II.

THE EARLY DAWN;
Or, Sketches of Christian Life in England in the Olden Time.

III.

DIARY OF MRS. KITTY TREVYLYAN:
A Story of the Times of Whitefield and the Wesleys.

Each 1 vol. large 12mo., ... $1 75
Or in sets, neatly bound and in boxes, . . 5 25

Fine Editions

Elegantly printed on tinted paper, bound
in extra cloth, beveled boards
and illustrated, $2 00.

MARY,

THE

HANDMAID OF THE LORD.

BY THE AUTHOR OF

"Schönberg-Cotta Family," "Early Dawn," "Diary of Kitty Trevylyan," etc., etc.

NEW YORK:
M. W. DODD, No. 506 BROADWAY.
1865.

EDWARD O. JENKINS, PRINTER, 20 NORTH WILLIAM ST. NEW YORK.

CONTENTS.

CHAPTER		PAGE
I.	THE MINISTRY OF ANGELS	15
II.	THE SALUTATION OF GABRIEL	49
III.	THE HANDMAID OF THE LORD	67
IV.	THE FRIENDSHIP OF THE COUSINS	91
V.	THE HOME AT NAZARETH.	111
VI.	MARY AMONG THE DISCIPLES	131
VII.	"SHE IS NOT DEAD, BUT SLEEPETH"	149

Ed avea in atto impressa esta favella
Ecce ancilla Dei, si propriamente
Come figura in cera si suggella.

PUBLISHER'S NOTE.

HE "Schönberg-Cotta Family," "The Early Dawn," and "Kitty Trevylyan,"* which we have sent into thousands of American households, will doubtless ensure a welcome reception to this volume, or to any thing that may hereafter appear from the same source.

The present work, which preceded in time of original issue those already named, was received from the author for publication here, but a few weeks since. Though quite in contrast,

---

* "Kitty Trevylyan" contains the special attraction of a Salutatory Note from the author to her readers on this side the Atlantic, designed for the double purpose of expressing her appreciation of the generous reception her works have had in this country, and her relations to us as her American publisher.

in some respects, with the productions which have made the "author of the Cotta Family" so widely known, it bears indisputable evidence of a like authorship, and will enlarge still more the circle of those coming under the charm of her genius and the purifying influence of her sentiments.

NEW YORK, *June,* 1865.

INTRODUCTION.

THE hours spent in writing this book have been very happy ones to me: may it lead others to the fountain from which the happiness of those hours flowed —to that Book, which, like Him of whom it testifies, is at once perfectly human and perfectly divine.

In disenthroning the mother of Jesus from the imaginary empire of heaven, have we not suffered ourselves to be robbed of much of the influence of the life of one of the lowliest and most blessed among the children of God? Errors are often best refuted, not by the manifestation of the contrary truth, but of the very truth from whose distortion they arose; and in the life of

Mary handmaid of the Lord, we may find the surest antidote to the adoration of Mary queen of Heaven.

Not that we may fill up a portrait with decided outlines and full colouring where the Scriptures only give us broken touches. It cannot be without meaning that but One Life in the New Testament is laid before us from infancy to the sepulchre. The silences of the Bible teach us scarcely less than its revelations and whilst we may affectionately gather and string together the few notices given us of Mary the mother of Jesus, it must not be forgotten that their very scarcity is among their most significant lessons.

On reviewing these pages, the fear has often come over me that it may be presumption to present them to others. Any representation we make of sacred things must, however unconsciously, contain so much of the darkness of our own confused and sinful hearts. The mirror is not only partial; it is marred, and broken, and distorted. And there are so many lessons which life alone can teach, that there must here be a thousand deficiencies which more experienced eyes will detect. I can only entreat the reader to pray that He, in whom alone is no darkness at all, would deign to use what there is of His light in these pages, and to forgive and render harmless their mistakes and deficiencies.

THE MINISTRY OF ANGELS.

Psalm ciii. 20.

Bless the Lord, ye his angels, that excel in strength, that do his commandments, hearkening to the voice of his word.

Daniel x. 13.

Michael, one of the chief princes, came and helped me.

Hebrews i. 14.

Are they not all ministering spirits, sent forth to minister for those who shall be heirs of salvation?

Revelations xxii. 8, 9.

I fell down to worship at the feet of the angel which shewed me these things. Then saith he unto me, See thou do it not; for I am thy fellow-servant.

I.

THE MINISTERING ANGELS.

IT is now eighteen hundred years since the heavens have been opened, save to the departing spirits they have received, or the eyes of men have been opened to see what lies nearer than the heavens, the host of God ministering to men; yet, during all these ages, not a day has passed in which the angels have not been doing God's pleasure—the pleasure of Him to whom the joy of saving sinful men was such that the shame of the cross was despised to obtain it, whose joy in a ransomed soul is such that the heart of a mother is appealed to as alone able to comprehend it: "She remembereth no more the anguish for the joy;" "He shall see of the travail of His soul, and shall be satisfied."

So long, while men have been writing biographies of each other and raising monuments, have the angels been at work in silence amongst us; bringing blessings with footsteps so soft that those who receive them, finding in the still chambers of the soul some heavenly gift, know not how it has come, but only whence, and, looking up, praise the Sender, while the messenger, perchance, stands by with folded wing and rejoices, and would have it even so.

Surely we might learn more from these ministers of heaven, these " elder sons of God," whom one day the children of the resurrection are to be like. Our spiritual world is too poor and empty. We do not exult enough in the wealth of our Creator. It is true that in the daylight the stars are hidden, but is it no joy to think the stars are there? In the city which has no need of the sun, myriads of " shining ones " can yet give light, and every precious stone has its part in mirroring the living ray.

It is He who has made the spring-morning, with its songs from hundreds of happy birds, its fragrance of thousands of flowers, each one perfect as a miniature—the fluttering of countless new-born leaves, each as with a separate joy—who has made heaven. It is He who pours out the abundance of beauty and life in the tropics, heaping into each summer month the harvests of a year, who has enriched the earth with such inward and outward stores of life and beauty, that every corner of it might be the study of a life-time—and yet declares the poorest human soul to be worth a world—it is He who has made the world we *cannot see,* the world which the eyes most versed in earth's beauty cannot picture, and the heart most enriched with earth's love and knowledge cannot conceive. Surely we do not fill our spiritual world half full enough. We do not heap the scale of glory as we should to overbalance the present suffering; and so this present time, with its cares and its disappointments, its losses and its work, weighs us down, and the vessel creeps heavily and lamely on; whereas if the weight of present trial, which it *must* bear, were balanced by the weight of coming glory which it *might, both* would help it on its homeward way.

There is with some of us a dread of such contemplation, as of something speculative. Let us have something, it is said, more practical. But is nothing practical but a precept?—the "do this" and "go thither?" Do we not acknowledge faith, that inward vision, as the root of all practice? Is not the Cross the fountain of more action than the Commandments? The fuel is around us in profusion; what we want is the fire. The cook is not the only practical labourer in preparing our food; but the reaper, the sower, the winds and rains of heaven, and the sunbeams shining because it is their nature to shine. Nothing is so practical as thought: our view of life moulds our life; our view of God moulds our souls; and the clearer and richer the spiritual world is to us, the more spiritual and heavenly, that is, the more practical and loving, the more full of high aims and lowly services, will our lives be.

Do we avail ourselves as we should of the true splendours of our faith, to throw into the shade the false glitter of the world, which is not of God? Do we not meet the aspirations after beauty and glory too much by silencing rather than by satisfying them? The gods of Greece, the ecclesiastical giant and fairy stories of the Middle Ages, are driven away by no mere negative iconoclasm; they are replaced by holier and more beautiful forms. "*His* train filleth the temple." The throne of God is no solitude. Nor need we fear the mingling in such high company will isolate us, or make the din of daily life, and this world's needful toil and traffic, sound doubly harsh. Heavenly exultation humbles, as heavenly joy expands the heart. Do we come from prayer, the highest of all communion, with a heart out of tune for the lowliest services in the home or by the sick-bed?—*then surely we have not prayed.* The angel of God thought it no humiliation to come from the presence of God to bear a message which might spare a pang to one innocent heart, and the first recorded ministry of an angel is to a slave.

In the Bible the angels are revealed to us in two ways: by glimpses in vision into their dwelling-place in heaven; by the unveiling of mortal eyes to behold their ministrations on earth. What a volume might be written on the *glimpses* of the Bible—those gleams of a clearer light and a diviner life than earth knows of, which show so plainly that the hand which revealed them is within the veil; that it is not an inhabitant of earth labouring to conceive, but an inhabitant of heaven stooping to utter what little mortals can comprehend of the infinite joy and glory he knows, but cannot tell.

Compare the sublimest, the most elaborate poetical descriptions of angels with the touches of the Bible, and we cannot but perceive the difference between the earthly picture and the heavenly revelation. Even Dante, the most seer-like of all poets, who "falls as a dead body falls" before the horror of the visions he has evoked, and in the imagined presence of his saintly Beatrice is constrained to utter in the face of ages that "yes" of penitence "so faint with fear and shame," that "to hear it you must have seen it;"—how feeble are his coloured portraits beside the broken outline of Isaiah!

The poet tells us that when he came out from the "dead air which had so saddened his eyes and heart," and his eyes began again to rejoice in the air "pure as the sweet colour of the Oriental sapphire," and he knew from far "the trembling of the sea," and bathed his hands and tear-stained cheeks "where the dew lay thickest because of the shade;" along "that sea which lay opposite Jerusalem," "there appeared to him a light moving so swiftly, that when for awhile he turned his eyes to inquire of Virgil what it was, he saw it larger and more brilliant." "Then from each side there appeared something white and defined, and little by little another white light came forth. And then as the white wings opened, and Virgil knew the heavenly pilot, he cried, 'Haste, haste; bend thy knees; behold the angel of

God; stretch forth thy hands; henceforth thou shalt see many such officers of the heavenly household.' See, he scorns all human aid, needs no oar, nor other sail than his wings between shores so distant. See, he turns them to heaven, striking the air with his eternal wings. And as the divine bird, the celestial pilot, came near, he became brighter, so that the eye could not sustain the radiance."

Compare this with the terrible glory of him whose countenance was like the lightning and his raiment white as snow; whose apparition made the Roman soldiers quake and become as dead men, but to whom the women, though affrighted, listened and grew calm, and returned with great joy, because he knew they sought Jesus. The shining garments and countenance like lightning had no terrors seen through the tears with which the Magdalen wept her Lord.

Compare the angels circling in mystic dances and wreaths of light in Dante's Paradise with Isaiah's vision of heaven; the glowing seraphim covering their faces and their feet with their wings, and crying as they flew, "Holy, holy, holy, Lord God of Hosts, the whole earth is full of thy glory." Not to speak of the sublimity of that unlaboured description, there is one element in all these Divine narratives distinctive above all others—the *moral* element; that awe of holiness which made the prophet cry, "Woe is me: for I am undone; because I am a man of unclean lips." It is not the mere radiance that dazzles him; it is the holiness, the majesty of purity.

Milton's angels, awful in holy beauty, and Bunyan's "shining ones," are too much steeped in Scriptural light to render contrast necessary, though even in Milton's Paradise we may see that his muse could not soar to the regions whence the Spirit of the prophet descended.

After Dante's angels comparison need scarcely descend to Tasso's ethereal spirit, "clothing his invisible form with air," "adorning his fair hair with rays," and poising his white wings tipped with gold on Lebanon." These super-spiritualized angels are very dim and unsatisfactory beings: the child's image of the beautiful winged spirits, or Dante's "divine bird," are better and truer and more poetical than all these angelic toilets. The old childish and Scriptural image will return again and again, however often expelled by the most logical arguments; after the utmost efforts at the conception of a form which is no form, and at hunting the subtle materialism through veil after veil of impalpable ether, the heart returns with loving obstinacy to the " young men in long white garments, sitting the one at the foot, the other at the head, where the body of Jesus had lain."

Nor is the reason in this matter at discord with the heart. Can we reverence too highly that human form which, in its humiliation, the Son of God assumed, and in its glory He now bears exalted on the right hand of the throne of God, far above all the angelic orders, and the principalities and the powers of heaven? Surely it was in a human form that the Son of God talked with Abraham and wrestled with Jacob; which, sword in hand, smote on the eyes of Joshua as the captain of the Lord's host; walked in the fiery furnace with the three faithful Jews; appeared to Daniel, the man greatly beloved, so that he became dumb, and no breath was left in him, and then touched him, and made him strong?

Ezek. i. 26–28 : " And above the firmament that was over their heads was the likeness of a throne, as the appearance of a sapphire stone: and upon the likeness of the throne was the likeness as the appearance of a man above upon it. And I saw as the colour of amber, as the appearance of fire round about within it; from the appearance of his loins even upward, and from the appearance of his loins even downward, I saw as it were the appearance of fire, and it had brightness round about. As the appearance of the bow that is in the cloud in the day of rain, so was the appearance of the brightness round about. This was the appearance of the likeness of the glory of the Lord. And when I saw it, I fell upon my face, and I heard a voice of one that spake." Dan. x. 5–7: "Then I lifted up mine eyes, and looked, and behold a certain man clothed in linen, whose loins were girded with fine gold of Uphaz: his body also was like the beryl, and his face as the appearance of lightning, and his eyes as lamps of fire, and his arms and his feet like in colour to polished brass, and the voice of his words like the voice of a multitude. And I Daniel alone saw the vision: for the men that were with me saw not the vision; but a great quaking fell upon them, so that they fled to hide themselves." Rev. i. 13–16: "And in the midst of the seven candlesticks one like unto the Son of man, clothed with a garment down to the foot, and girt about the paps with a golden girdle. His head and his hairs were white like wool, as white as snow; and his eyes were as a flame of fire; and his feet like unto fine brass, as if they burned in a furnace; and his voice as the sound of many waters. And he had in his right hand seven stars; and out of his mouth went a sharp two-edged sword; and his countenance was as the sun shineth in his strength."

This is surely no coincidence of conception, but an identity of vision—a vision of Him who was in the beginning with God, and was God, in the bosom of the Father, yet delighting in the habitable parts of His earth; the eternal manifestation of the eternally invisible; the revelation of Him who dwelleth in the unapproachable light, whom no eye hath seen nor can see; the eternal Son of the eternal Father; in whose image were made the sons of God and the seraphim; the Angel Gabriel, who standeth in the presence of God; Michael, one of the chief princes; those glorious beings whose countenances are as light and whose raiment white as snow; and Adam the holy keeper of Eden, "which was the son of God"—in whose glorious image (He having taken the shame of our fallen and mortal humanity), the fainting, suffering, and wayfaring Christians around us here, shall one day shine. Restored man will be restored after a type existing before the sons of God shouted for joy at the foundation of this world; and our confidence for the future of redeemed humanity, our deliverance from that melancholy dread that a subsequent race will supplant ours, as the tree-eaters and fish-lizards of the old world have been supplanted, and the human race become a fossil formation for the study of a new order of geologizing angels, rests not merely on the promise of the resurrection and on the present existence in heaven of Jesus, Son of Mary and Son of God, which have been so beautifully adduced in refutation,* but on the conviction that this human form, now so humbled and debased by sin and suffering, was the earliest and most glorious type of creature existence.

Let us picture the angels, since we can think of no existence without picturing it, as children picture them, and as Abraham and Mary Magdalen saw them, and dwell on what is told us of their heavenly dwelling-place and their earthly ministrations.

Their dwelling-place. It is a palace; for the throne of God is there. It is a temple; for

* Hugh Miller's "Old Red Sandstone."

God himself and the Lamb are there. It is a home; for the Father and the Son are there, and the angels are sons. It is a palace full of festival; they shout for joy." It is a home full of activity; " they do His pleasure." It is a temple full of song; for they say with a loud voice, " Worthy is the Lamb that was slain." Somewhere in this material creation, heaven now exists. Astronomers may have gazed from afar upon its crystal walls: it may lie in that undiscovered centre, around which these countless systems of worlds circle in mystic dance like the spirits in Dante's Paradise. For be this universe but a thought or idea of God existing only in Him, to man it is a real universe; and to perplex ourselves as to whether it is an idea or an external form, seems much like children disputing about the materials of which their letters are composed, instead of learning to read them. At this moment, whilst we are toiling and trifling here, *heaven exists*—a place, a palace, a temple, a home; and the angels are rejoicing there with holy reverence and rapture.

Their numbers are spoken of as defying number: "Ten thousand times ten thousand, and thousands of angels;" "legions of angels;" " the hosts of God." They are not merely a company, an army, a kingdom; but a race, a creation.

Their order. Many fanciful things have been written on the subject, but the existence of subordination of rank among them is evident; subordination without envy, and supremacy without pride. For how can pride exist, or envy, where, beyond all the joy of command, is the joy of service, and the highest distinction is to stand in the presence of God?

Their occupations. And this leads us to their ministrations and their warfare. Among their hosts but two forms are brought forward into individual distinctness: Gabriel, who stands in the presence of God, and Michael, one of the chief princes. Of the ages of the life of Michael, two incidents are revealed to us; both are incidents of warfare, and warfare concerning man. He stood by the Son of man in that mysterious contest with the evil powers, which delayed for three weeks the answer to Daniel's prayers; and "disputing with the Devil about the body of Moses, he durst not bring against him a railing accusation." For, strange as it sounds, there has been, as we are told there will be, war in heaven. The two aspects in which the angels are represented to us are as messengers and as warriors.

Before the creation of man there had been a fall. Among the morning stars which sang together at the creation, one son of the morning bore no light. Though heaven is so peopled with rejoicing hosts, myriads who once rejoiced and praised God there, sing and rejoice no more for ever. Concerning that fall, Milton tells us a great deal more than the Bible; yet the Bible tells us more than we sometimes think. *How* they fell, with none to tempt and heaven to lose, with a nature undimmed by the flesh and unenfeebled by sin, looking upon God and dwelling in His smile; fell from the height of angelic sanctity, to the depth of utter malignity, from the joy of accepted service, to rebellion without hope and remorse without repentance; how can it be possible, with fierce passion and exhaustless ingenuity, to continue a warfare whose stratagems are ceaselessly baffled, and whose successes are but so many fresh pangs added to the anguish which *they know* is to torment them in its time—human nature retains too little of its original strength, and too much of its original goodness, to conceive.

What form they bear, we can also but dimly

imagine. It is remarkable that Satan is not spoken of in the Bible as having a human form, although he is said to transform himself into an angel of light; and what is hideous and loathsome, is as essentially associated with sin as beauty with holiness. There may be more than a typical meaning in the terms, "old serpent," "dragon," "as a lion." It may be that the human form, which reigns and rejoices in heaven, will not be tormented in the lake of fire; but however this be, it is surely a blessed fact, that beauty and truth are essentially one, and can but temporarily be divorced.

But the fact of that fall is recorded in the Bible, and reflected in many a reversed and broken and distorted image from the turbid waters of old Pagan legend. Does it not reverberate in confused and broken echoes—a tone multiplied into a chord, and chords jarred into discords—from the icy hell of the North; from the Dragon conflicts of many religions; from the lifeless rock where Prometheus, "lover of men," cursed and defied the gods, and repeated the old lie of Eden, that God was iron-hearted, and he, the heroic sufferer, overborne by might but not by justice, lay bound for the divine gift he would have won for men, to make them as gods—that ideal of god-defying endurance of superhuman woe, of which the old world made its heroes, and Milton his Satan?

For us the terrible tragedy opens at Eden, and we cannot penetrate beyond—the combatants, angels and devils, armies from which a legion can be spared to one point in the contest—the battle-field, heaven, the air around us, with the prince of its powers, the earth we tread, where Satan walks to and fro, and angels minister, and more fearful than all, *our own souls;* the weapons on our side, faith, hope, peace and prayer, on the side of the enemy, "*lies;* lies about God, about the world, about ourselves. For this warfare continues unabated yet, though long since the death-blow was given on a Cross, and the song of triumph sung around an opened grave.

The Son of God " beheld Satan as lightning fall from heaven." To what point in the conflict of ages He alluded, we know not, nor from how many such falls the enemy may have reared his desperate head; but we know that the Apostle Paul fought still against wicked spirits in heavenly places; and John, carried forward in spirit to the end, beheld the expulsion of the Accuser, who accused the brethren night and day, rejoiced over as a fresh triumph. Yes, we may not close our eyes to the fact, that the battle rages unabated yet, that whatever fallen angels are " delivered into chains of darkness, reserved for judgment," and whenever these fell, myriads, and above all he who is the leader of them all, still go up and down in the earth, as in the days of Job, seeking " whom they may devour ;" accusing the brethren in that Presence into which the Forerunner has for us entered ; accusing God in those hearts in which the Spirit of God, as in a temple, dwells.

No personified principle of evil, but a person, as really a person as the Son of God, as Gabriel, as each of us, is opposed to us children of the dust, children of the day ; and, under him, spirits as desperate and malignant as he. His mighty intellectual power and experience we may be sure even Milton's Satan does not adequately portray ; nor Goethe's Mephistopheles, his revolting wickedness, his base cunning, and his mocking defiance of God. For more than five thousand years he has studied human nature with the terrible earnestness of hatred and envy, of a baffled foe, and a lost soul, and with the science of an angel. He came into Eden, and tempted Eve to believe that the God, who had made man in all the freshness of new life, and in all the fullness of mature life, had planted Paradise for him, and brought her to Adam—who had talked with them and blessed them—*envied* His creatures. He tempted Adam, through God's best gift, to rebel against the Giver; and ever since there has not been a lie too base for him to utter or too absurd for man to believe about God—not a heavenly gift which he has not tempted us to abuse or spoil. And on that day, that Holy Day in heaven, when the "sons of God" came to present themselves before God, the adversary, the outcast, unscared by the holiness or the abhorrence of angels, or by the bitter memory of his ancient state, came among them to accuse a faithful child of God to his father; and ever since he has accused the brethren—alas! how easy an indictment—and hindered and grieved them night and day. With all his subtlety, how blind! with all his strength, how powerless! Does he not know, that out of all these furnaces the tried come, not weak and marred, but stronger and more beautiful; that all his fires are but purifying the heavenly gold, and bringing out tint after tint in the celestial portrait ; that he is but enamelling likenesses of the Son of God ? Does he not know that in the heaven where he accuses, Jesus pleads, the Lord our Righteousness ; and from the shield of faith on earth, every fiery dart but rebounds in music—quenched indeed for the believer, but for him how fearfully reserved, when the time shall come!

But whatever he knows, we know he ventured to tempt the Holy One himself, tempted the Son of God to tempt the Father, tempted the Holy and Almighty One to worship *him*, so blind is his cunning or so daring his despair.

And we know it was not with scorn or with superhuman might the Saviour in His sinless humanity met the Evil One, but with the words of God, with self-denying trust, with lowly obedience, with reverent worship towards the living God.

Our example, Jesus endured this for us—one of those hours, whose full bitterness we can never know, unless we could know the purity of the Tempted—what it was for Him who had dwelt from the beginning in the bosom of the Father and left it to save fallen man, to endure the presence of the enemy of God and man ; for Him who knew no sin, to whom sin was loathsome beyond the most loathsome sight from which we turn shuddering away, to be tempted by the author of all sin ; for the Life to be assailed by him who brought death into the world ; for the Truth to endure the taunts of the father of lies, and to meet it, not with the might of one blasting word, but in weakness and humiliation, in all (save the sympathy of a fallen nature) as we meet him. And this as our example : He endured for us! The cross, the scornful gaze of multitudes, He has strengthened others to endure for Him and rejoice, but this He only could have borne, this and those two other hours of agony when the weight of the coming strife lay heavy on Him, and He was sore amazed—and when He bound our sin and curse around His very soul, and was forsaken of God. Yes, there " it was finished"—the Tempter is vanquished, and his days are numbered, the Accuser was silenced, the triumph was begun, the issue of the conflict was openly proclaimed to heaven and earth and hell, and there only, at the foot of that Cross, have any ever since overcome.

More wonderful than that he stole into Eden, or ventured into heaven, is it that Satan should dare to struggle after the Resurrection of the

Lord. Yet we know he has not ceased, and we see it. We see it, alas! not only in our victories, but in his; in a world where heathenism deifies evil, if not the Evil One himself, in the scoffs of infidelity, in the dreams of counterfeit Christianity, in a Church without visible unity, divided against itself, and not discerning or looking for its Lord, in controversies amongst brethren, in enmity amongst those our Lord deigns to call His friends, in love grown cold —in our own lives to-day and yesterday do we see no traces of his evil power, hindering good works, imbittering good things and sweetening evil, or are all such traces trophies? They might be; but *are they?* Nay, all are waiting, " the whole creation" groaneth for deliverance, angels are waiting whilst they minister, heaven is waiting while it praises, hell is waiting and rebelling; let us also wait and watch, wait in working and in prayer. To the warfare which strains the powers of legions of fallen angels, and exercises the full energies of Michael and those who excel in strength, we, the weakest, and yet in the van and thick of the fight, should not surely come with slumbering or unarmed hearts, remembering what a victory is possible and what strength is promised to the feeblest hand which grasps the cross, or clings to the Crucified. Let us be strong and of good courage, the Apostles and early martyrs fought a good fight and won the crown, and the Lord is as near and salvation nearer than then. In the last great battle all evil powers will be cast out for ever, and in that home which our Saviour is preparing, that city in which all who love Him shall dwell, there shall enter nothing that defileth, nor maketh a *lie*, for ever and ever.

Not only are we fellow-soldiers with the angels, but fellow-servants. From their warfare it is joyful to turn to their ministry.

Twice only in the Old Testament do we read of the angelic swords being turned against men ; the angel whom David saw between earth and heaven, with a drawn sword in his hand stretched out over Jerusalem, from whom the four sons of Araunah hid themselves, whose sword was stayed in mercy on the site of the future temple ; and the angel, who in the camp of the Assyrians smote in one night one hundred fourscore and five thousand, and in the morning they were all dead corpses. In the Apocalypse, the allusion to such angelic agency in judgment, in the final agony of this age, is constant: how far providential judgments of famine and pestilence are executed now by such personal agency, we know not. Probably when our eyes are opened, we shall find the universe infinitely fuller of life than we ever dreamed, and behold many a dead material law transformed into the service of a conscious spirit. Hands are more wonderful instruments than power-looms, and He who can create life has no need of mechanism.

To the manifestations of *one angel*, " the Angel of the Lord" in the Old Testament, we must approach with awe, because as we gaze on the glorious vision, it expands and glows into a majesty beyond that of any created being, and with Hagar we must say, " I have looked on Him who liveth and seeth me," the Self-existent and Omniscient; with Abraham, " Behold I have taken upon me to speak unto the Lord, which am but dust and ashes ;" with Jacob, " The Lord is in this place, and I knew it not" (compare Gen. xxxi. 11–13, xxviii. 16, xlviii. 16) ; with Joshua, " The place whereon we stand is holy ;" with Manoah, " We have seen God." He whose name was a " secret" from Israel, and " wonderful" to Manoah, the angel which redeemed Jacob from all evil, the Angel of God's presence who saved His people, is surely One beyond Gabriel and Michael, One before whom every knee shall ere long bow in heaven and in earth; the Angel of the Covenant—even Christ the Lord; He who is with God, One with Him, and with His Church, one with her; One in whom we can wonder at no depth of love nor height of power. But the two angels who "went on to Sodom," and sought Lot in the midst of the corrupt city, and hastened him, when the morning of doom arose, and, as he yet lingered, laid hold of his hand, and upon the hand of his wife, and upon the hand of his two daughters, "the Lord being merciful unto him"—these who were thus eager for the rescue of one soul, and that one soul so wavering and earthly, were surely among the ministering spirits.

Three manifestations of angels, the only ones which remain to be alluded to, in the Old Testament, are peculiarly interesting, because they seem to be not so much the mission of a special messenger as the opening of mortal eyes to an agency perpetually, though invisibly and silently, at work around us. The angel which checked Balaam; the hosts of God which met Jacob; the chariots of Israel and the horsemen thereof, to which the eyes of the trembling servant of Elisha were opened, 2 Kings vi. 15–18.

This last is surely one of the most precious incidents of angelic ministrations revealed in the Old Testament. It seems to show us the angels at their ordinary work, not in the state garments of the direct heavenly embassy, but in their every-day apparel, at their daily tasks. The daily garb, how glorious, horses and chariots of fire! This work, how lowly and how gracious. "Round about Elisha." Watching, guarding night and day—" the Angel of the Lord encampeth round about them that fear Him, and delivereth them." In the solitary sick-chamber, in the home of bereavement, on messages of mercy in the dark alleys of our cities, in the workshop where one heart prays, in the prisons where even now some of us lie bound for Christ; in the lowly mission-station among the wilds of the untamed West or the hostile crowds of the degenerate East, by the cradles of infants, by the beds of dying believers, what companies are gathered, what eyes are watching, what hearts are loving, what hands are ministering.

But at length the long suspense ceased, as all waitings will one day; the hope of ages was to be fulfilled, and messengers of glad tidings came from God to man. There was no earthquake among the hills of Galilee, no tumult among the dwellings of Jerusalem; to one priest ministering at evening in the temple by the altar of incense, an old man and childless; to one maiden in Galilee, on whom the serious hopes of life were opening, the Angel Gabriel came—to both with blessing, to both with the gentle command, "Fear not," tempering the awe of the heavenly visitation. The Joy of heaven came and dwelt on earth, and the world knew Him not; He came unto His own and His own received Him not: but the angels knew Him. To them the message of His birth was "glad tidings of great joy;" Jesus in the manger, as on the throne above the sapphire firmament, was Christ the Lord—and a multitude of the heavenly host filled the night with light and song, praising God, and saying, "Glory to God in the highest, and on earth peace, good will toward men."

Twice afterwards are we told of their ministrations to the Saviour on earth; twice only amidst the desertion of earth and the enmity of hell, was one from among the myriads of those obedient adoring hosts permitted to approach the Son of man. In the wilderness, when Satan left Him, after those long days of hunger and those hours of temptation, the angels came and ministered unto Him; and in the garden when one drop of the bitter cup might not pass from Him, nor the agony be abated, yet the prayer of the Son was heard, and there appeared unto Him an angel strengthening Him. The women of Galilee had ministered unto Him; from the woman of Samaria He had asked for a draught of cold water, but among the armies which He rules the myriads who veil their faces round His throne, or fly on any errand at His word, there is *one* who can remember an hour in which the Son of God emptied of His glory, and neglected by His redeemed, was strengthened by His creature.

By the cross we hear nothing of the angels; Mary was there close at hand, and John, and some watched from afar; but in that hour of man's darkest sin, and his redemption, and the Son of God's desertion, when the sun was darkened, and the rocks rent, it is not revealed to us what the angels felt.

But around the opened sepulchre, we find the joyful forms again, young with the youth whose freshness ages cannot dim, rolling away the stone with an earthquake, and watching where the body of Jesus had lain, giving messages of comfort to the women, and to Mary Magdalen, who, they knew, sought Jesus, appearing in a form so human, and speaking in tones so gentle, that it seems scarcely to have aroused her, when she heard the angelic question, "Woman, why weepest thou?"

With what inconceivable joy must those words have been uttered, "*He is not here, He is risen!*" to the disciples indeed glad tidings of great joy, but to the angels a song of triumph echoing through all ages and all worlds.

One more message of deliverance, when the iron prison-gates opened of themselves before the Angel-guide of Peter; and another, when by Paul, in the night, on the tempest-tossed ship, "when neither sun nor stars had for many days appeared," and all hope was taken away, the Angel of God stood with the promise of rescue, and the history of angel ministrations to man closes.

But their ministry has not ceased; they are at work among us still; and how often we may meet their hosts, or be guarded by the fiery chariots, or be checked or strengthened by *one angel* sent from heaven, we shall not know, until in that future whose rest will be no sleep, and whose service no toil, where all of earth shall have vanished, save those works of love which God never forgets, we may discover friends perchance among the heavenly host, and find the history of earthly trial and toil no strange tale in heaven.

One thing however is certain. No temper so assimilates us with devils as envy; none to the angels so much as love; no act is so like Satan as to tempt; no act so like the angels as self-forgetting, self-denying service of others. If in hearing of the fall of a brother, however differing or severed from us, we feel the least inclination to linger over it instead of hiding it in grief and shame, or veiling it in the love which covereth a multitude of sins; if in seeing a joy or a grace, or an effective service given to others and not to us, we do not rejoice, but feel depressed, let us be very watchful: the most diabolical of passions may mask itself as humility or zeal for the glory of God. Let us watch and pray, for the Evil One is very strong and very near: yet let us be of good courage, for nearer and stronger is Jesus, the Holy One of God.

And there is one thing in which our Master

has given us an honour the angels cannot have; "He took not on Him the nature of angels, but the seed of Abraham," and we have to minister amidst weakness, temptation, and reproach; we can comfort others with the comfort *wherewith we ourselves have been comforted of God.*

And ever let us remember that Jesus has said with His suffering Church, "Why persecutest thou Me?" and with His succoured brethren, "Ye have done it unto Me;" so that we also, as well as that one angel in Gethsemane, are permitted, are commanded, to minister unto the Lord.

THE SALUTATION OF GABRIEL.

Luke i. 28.

Hail, thou that art highly favoured, the Lord is with thee: blessed art thou among women.

II.

THE SALUTATION OF GABRIEL.

GOD'S religion begins with that to which man's religions tend — the favour and presence of God. Man ends with aspirations; God begins with gifts. When the angel came to Mary in her Galilean home, his first words were of grace: "Hail! thou that art highly favoured, graciously accepted, filled with grace. Blessed art thou among women!" And the fullness of the blessing is contained in the announcement of the fact, "The Lord is with thee." Afterwards came a promise which made her destiny a more glorious one than ever had fallen, or ever can fall, to the lot of woman; most glorious in this, that, like all the glory which God gives, it absorbed self instead of magnifying it; a promise for which, since Eve, mother of all living, rejoiced in her first-born (little dreaming that the first infant smile earth saw was on the face of a fratricide), faithful hearts had yearned and waited, and in whose fulfillment all generations shall indeed "call her blessed."

And yet that first salutation of the angel, that first blessing, that actual fact—"the Lord is with thee"—transcends all promises; for in it lies the secret of all strength and the germ of eternal joy. Heaven's richest blessings are its widest; beyond all the wine of individual bliss is the living water of which all may drink abundantly and live.

The Lord, the Almighty, He who fainteth not, neither is weary; whose understanding there is no searching, of whose riches the whole earth, and of whose glory the heavens are full—*with thee*, on thy side against all foes, by thy side in all thy sorrows; with thee as no friend, as no angel, can be with thee; with thine inmost spirit, with thee as thy light, thy strength, thy joy, thy life, thy Redeemer, thy Father!

This is *the secret*, hidden from the wise and revealed unto babes—the truth that when we perceive we live, when we forget we wither and droop, when we remember we are in health and abound.

The presence of God in grace with the individual soul, *God with us*, this is life; the conscious abiding in his presence, *we with God*, this is health. And this is what the Gospel alone proclaims to the world, and the Spirit of God alone can reveal to the heart.

The natural religion of man, whether outwardly developed in a creed or system or not, consists in the effort of the heart to toil up to God, combined with the struggle of the conscience to interpose something between.

These aspirations may vary from the most ingenious corporeal self-torture of the ascetic to the most beneficent works of a refined deism, or the most spiritual exercises and emotions of natural devotion. The path may be made as rough as conscience can dictate, or rich in all the luxury of artistic beauty which warm hearts and poetical fancies can shed upon it; but unless it begins with God, it can never lead to God.

The favour of God, the perfect acceptance of the soul by God, is not the end of spiritual life, but its very element and commencement. This is what human systems never teach. They can fill the temple with incense, and the altar with offerings, the heart with a glow of emotion, and the life with the fervour of benevolence; for human nature has not sunk to the moral level of Satan's, or he need not tempt: the thistles have not yet choked the flowers; the ruin retains a thousand relics of its old design and decorations, and it is the ruin of a temple of God. On the wings of enrapt devotion or poetic thought, men seek to soar to heaven; by the roughest ladders of spiritual exercise and self-renunciation, they strive one by one to climb the heights, and they have built Babels to make the access easy for the multitude. But "*no man hath ascended up to heaven but He who came down from heaven, even the Son of man which is in heaven*"—in heaven and with Nicodemus.

Thus one effort of human religions, the endeavour to find or make a Way to God, is met and fulfilled in Jesus. He is the Way. The heaven we seek, toiling over rock and mountain, yet finding it ever hopelessly above, is at our doors — " the heavens" *do* " touch the earth," " the *there*" is " *here*."* We have found

* " Ach kein Steg will dahin führen,
Ach, der Himmel über mir
Will die Erde nie berühren
Und das Dort is niemals hier.

Read this poem of Schiller's (*Der Pilgrim*) with that Name which is above every name as its solution.

Jesus; we have found God. Jesus is our religion, our offering, the incense of our offering, our Sacrament, our Priest. God himself is the way to God. Immanuel, " the Lord is with thee !"

Side by side with the heavenward aspirations of the heart, we find the conscience equally hard at work to keep God away, or at least to interpose some veil or shield between us and Him. The one feeling is as truthful as the other. The one arises from a sense of exile from God's presence, the other from a sense of unfitness for it; the first from a dim thirst for life, the last from a dim fear of justice. The veil may be woven of the roughest material texture, or the subtlest spiritual essence. The apron and the trees of the garden have passed through an endless variety of forms, yet the original materials have been little departed from. A robe of our own weaving to enwrap the soul, and a hiding-place amidst God's creation from the Creator. Sweet natural affections, heroic virtues, unnatural renunciations, man has wrapped around the deformity of his fallen soul. Multitudes of monstrous symbolic ideas, gorgeous religious ceremonials, the very beauty of the earth and the glory of the heavens God made for us, the very ordinances He gave to make us remember Him, the angels who delight to do His pleasure, the just spirits He has made perfect, she who in her lowliness was honoured to be the mother of her Lord— of all these have we made screens behind which to hide from God, dreaming with Adam that God's light, like the sun's, casts a shadow, and that there can be a barrier not translucent to Him. Yet Adam's conscience and the natural conscience of mankind are right; it is perfectly true that we cannot stand in the light of God's presence—we need a veil and a hiding-place.

And here in our guilt, as well as in our exile, God meets us. All human ways to Him lead not to Him; they are indeed not ways, but barriers. *Jesus is the way.* All our screens from God are no refuges; they hide indeed His light from us, but leaving us exposed to Him. *Jesus is the hiding-place;* in Him our transgressions are forgiven, our sins are covered. The Omniscient Eye, which is in itself light as well as sight, sees not a sin in us looking on us through Him; and "The Lord is with thee" becomes again to redeemed man the joyful truth it is to unfallen angels.

From Adam's "For he was afraid," to David's

"In the secret of Thy presence shalt thou hide them ;" from Peter's "Depart from me, for I am a sinful man, O Lord," to "Then were the disciples glad when they saw the Lord ;" what a change! The Lord our Righteousness makes the name Immanuel glad tidings of great joy.

And from this reception of Jesus, from the belief of this fact, God the Saviour with us, how many other joyful facts and blessed duties flow! It is this which is the strength and joy of the Christian ; it is the feebler or fuller apprehension of this which makes the difference between one disciple and another ; for do not all the various compounds of Christian character, when thoroughly analyzed, depend on the relative proportions of this one ingredient?

The presence of God! Let us ponder in the silence of our hearts what it means, and what it involves. It is the deepest joy of heaven. In all the pictures our imagination can draw of heaven, in all the glimpses faith obtains of its inconceivable happiness, the perfection of every faculty, the constant and successful employment of every energy with an intensity we reach here but in a few fervent moments, in the praises of that temple whose ordinary worshippers are poets and whose ordinary language dwells in the heights of song, of whose joy we know so little except negatively—by the absence of tears and pain and sin—the joy of joys is, not the myriads of angels, the light, the activity, the song, but that *the Lord is there!* "God and the Lamb are the light thereof." And this, even this, is ours by faith now; ours with one element which angels cannot know; ours as restored exiles and forgiven prodigals, as the presence of a reconciled Father and a Redeemer crucified for us.

Then what results from this?

In the first place, we are never alone. The Christian's life should never, can never, be a solitary one. A life of service must be a life of love. And no path can be barren, if the fountain of living waters flows by its side. Yet there are lives which bereavement has left very poor in natural companionship, and homes which at times seem silent when the echo of other full and joyous firesides reaches them. And there are those who have no homes on earth, dwelling as strangers in the homes of others; and in all lives there are lonely hours, hours when trial and perplexity come, and the friend on whose sympathy and judgment we would lean is not near; and in many hearts there are places too tender for any human hand to touch. What a truth then is that which turns hours of loneliness into hours of the richest and most blessed companionship; companionship which makes the heart glow and the face shine, so that those who dwell much in it, bear a visible and sensible sunshine with them wherever they come. For the presence of God is no abstract truth, no mere presence of a sun, to whose light we may lay open our souls as the flowers their leaves, and be transfigured; but the communion of spirit with spirit; no mere presence of an angel watching us and loving us in silence—it is the presence of One with whom we may have intercourse as a man with his friend, to whom we may speak—speak of everything which interests us, make requests and have them granted, ask questions and have them answered; One who is not silent toward us. Oh, let us bathe our souls in this joy—drink, yea, drink abundantly of it, and be refreshed! Let us begin every prayer remembering it, and rise from every prayer strengthened with the remembrance; read the Bible as the word of One present; speak of Him as of One present; carry it with us all day as our shield and strength, and rest in it all night.

And not only are we thus never lonely, never without sympathy, but we are never without help. We have no right to say of any good work, It is too hard for me to do; or of any sorrow, It is too hard for me to bear; or of any sinful habit, It is too hard for me to overcome. St. Peter knew what it was when he felt the hand stretched out to grasp his, and walked on the waves. St. Paul knew what it meant when he said, "I have learned both how to be abased and how to abound; in whatever state I am, I have learned to be content; I can do all things through Christ, which strengtheneth me."

We know the power of a day's or an hour's intercourse with one thoroughly and intensely in earnest; the expansion it gives to our thoughts, the reality it gives to our lives, the lifting up of our whole natures by the might of sympathy to a higher level and a clearer air. What then is it to dwell perpetually in the presence of Him whose purposes are facts, whose words are creations, with whom no falsehood can exist an instant; in living communion with the Highest, the Mightiest and the Best? It is to have our hearts permanently raised into their purest atmosphere, and our minds permanently expanded to their fullest vigour; it is daily to grow like God.

Then, how free this truth makes us! What are the glances of men when the eye of God is on us, and our eye on Him! What does the opinion of the whole world, or, what is to us far weightier, the felt and expressed opinion of our own small public, the circle in which we move, weigh in that balance? As sympathy, indeed, much; but as a fetter, light as St. Peter's chains when the angel touched him.

Yet, in this freedom, how humble! Seen through and through, not a broken resolution, not an infirmity, not a sin, not a desire, a regret, a fear, a mixed motive unknown! A presence we could not stand in one single instant, if the light which penetrates us did not also clothe us, and the God who sees us were not also the Man who was accursed for us.

Yet if these things be so, how is it the Church is not indeed a light set on a hill, from which men may indeed fly as they do from the light of the world, but which they cannot open their eyes and fail to see? How is it that the life of every one among us is not such that all men should be constrained to say of us, as of our Lord, We find no fault in them?

Is it not because, though God is always with us, we are so seldom with God? There is a sense in which, if any man keep the words of Jesus, the Father and the Son *come* to him, and manifest themselves to him as they do not unto the world; a sense as little contradictory of the truth of his perpetual presence with all, as it is of astronomical fact, when in common speech we say, The sun rises and sets.

It is possible for us on earth consciously to abide in God's presence, and it is possible for us not to do so, and in not doing so, unchanging as His love and purposes are, to loose the enjoyment of every blessing which His presence brings; to be and do the very reverse of all our Lord says of the fruitful branch; to bear no fruit; to dishonour the Father; to wither and dry up; to be cast forth as a branch and burned—all the works and toil of our life (some of them perhaps religious works) burned and reduced to ashes; and we, if still, in His abounding grace, saved though as by fire, yet meeting Him who laid down His life for us, without one of those labours of love He so rejoices never to forget.

And, on the other hand, it is possible so to abide in Him, so consciously to dwell in His presence, as in an atmosphere of perpetual prayer, that, having in ourselves neither strength nor peace, we may yet, through living union with Him, bring forth much fruit ; have in Jesus, and in ourselves through the indwelling Spirit, a perpetual fountain of life and peace, and be to others a perpetual source of refreshment and blessing. May He engrave His warnings in their full depth upon our hearts, and enable us to aim steadfastly at the highest things, and covet earnestly the best gifts ; and, in spite of repeated failure and forgetfulness, to rest satisfied with nothing short of this—that as to each of us it is said, "The Lord is with thee," so we even here may be " ever with the Lord."

It is no elaborate picture that we are commanded to form, no laboured realization we are required painfully to affect; we are but to lift up our eyes, and we shall surely meet His eye resting upon us ; lift them up, not only in our prayers, but at our work, amidst our cares, our perplexities, our sorrows, and our joys. We do not leave His presence to enter on His service. Mary the sister of Martha was as much in communion with Jesus when she anointed His feet with precious ointment, as when she sat at His feet and heard His words. When the people of God journeyed through the wilderness, the pillar of fire journeyed before them; and when Israel dwelt in tents, the Shechinah shone within a tabernacle. And by-and-by, we know not how soon, all our struggles will cease; our eyes will no more close heavy with sleep, even when Jesus transfigured is nigh; the world will be able to distract our thoughts no more, nor Satan to weave his magic veils before our dazzled sight. Then the joy of heaven will be but the sight of what we now by faith possess—we shall see Him as He *is;* and the glory of heaven will but be the visible revelation of what we may now by faith enjoy. "When He appears, then shall we appear with Him in glory."

But in the future, let us not loose sight of the present blessing, nor forget, in the hope of the full redemption, the glorious Earnest of the inheritance actually bestowed on faith. In the living temples of God now, as it is reported of the old temple at Jerusalem, and prophecied of that holy city which shall be one temple, God himself being its sanctuary, a well of living water springs up perpetually unto eternal life. The moral strength which God gives to the believer is no mere nourishment and bracing of the spiritual faculties, but the indwelling of the living Spirit, of One who may be "grieved," but whose nature is "love, joy, peace," since such are the visible tokens of His presence. As personally as Jesus will be present with the Church after the resurrection, the Holy Spirit is present with her now. Here, indeed, sin often dims our perceptions and hinders our communion; but God is the same to us now as He will be hereafter, and what will heaven be but the manifestation, to purified and perfected beings, of the love and the presence of God?

THE HANDMAID OF THE LORD.

Luke I.

Behold the handmaid of the Lord.

III.

THE HANDMAID OF THE LORD.

AND Mary said, "Behold the handmaid of the Lord; be it unto me according to thy word." The announcement of the angel did not fill her heart with the exultation of a destiny loftier than any ever to be given to woman. To be the mother of God's Anointed, of man's Saviour; to have the lips, which shall one day call the dead to resurrection, call her mother; to see the eyes on which angels wait, before which devils tremble, raised to hers with the dependent love of a child—this promise, for which queens would have resigned their crowns as dust, by which earth's proudest ambitions are dull as faded gilding, exalted her not; it bowed her heart in the lowliest prostration. Her feeling was not so much exultation as submission; not the magnifying of self, but the joyful yielding up of self to God. In its measure all true joy is humbling. In the day of a fulfilled hope we could joyfully embrace an enemy and minister to a beggar; but with heavenly joy it is ever essentially thus. It is so deep, it is so free, it is so undeserved.

And before passing on to the subject of service in general, let us pause an instant to gather into a focus the scattered rays, and picture to ourselves, as far as we can, Mary, the handmaid of the Lord.

Not that we want an "Imitation of Mary" as a companion to the "Imitation of Christ." Only one perfect example has appeared on earth for woman as well as man. But whilst the domestic history of so many mothers and daughters of modern times has been written for our example, and so many sweet family portraits have been engraved for the benefit of the Church, we surely need not fear to study affectionately and reverently the likeness of Mary, the mother of our Lord.

If Humility were to descend incarnate upon earth, would many of us recognize her? Not with eyes cast down, not in a robe of penitence, not pale and fasting, moving slow and soberly, with a demure sadness in her countenance; but with eyes turned trustfully heavenwards (though often glistening with tears, since the humility of the sinning and redeemed cannot be that of the unfallen), with the smile of a happy child on her lips, with the glow of joy and health on her face, her head garlanded with the wild flowers God caused to spring in her path, her step light and free as childhood's—refusing no good gift from above, shrinking from no appointed office, whether on a throne or in a hospital,—would she be understood? Yet in such a portrait may we not see many features of her to whom Gabriel came from God? Or rather, since no Christian grace grows singly, and although we may break the sunbeam into the prism, the light of heaven must always contain all the colours, love (the true ray of heat) being never absent—do we often find them more purely blended than in the few glimpses given us of the character of Mary?

There is no disclaiming of God's gifts, no doubting of His promise, no shrinking from that burden of honour. She did not say with Moses, " O my Lord, send now, I pray Thee, by the hand of him whom Thou shouldst send ;" or with Gideon, " *If* Thou wilt save Israel by me, as Thou has said, . . . let me prove me now this once with the fleece ;" or with Isaiah, " Woe is me, for I am undone;" or with Jeremiah, "O my Lord God, I am but a child;"—she knew it all; knew that she was poor and of low degree, not merely a little below this honour, but altogether and infinitely beneath it. Her whole song shows this; but she knew also that with God no miracle of power or grace is impossible. Because in herself she was nothing, she could rejoice in God her Saviour; she could frankly acknowledge that God had done to her great things. Her humility was not that morbid self-depreciation, that compound of vexed pride and unbelief, which so often takes its name—depreciating God's talents as well as our services; but having its root in faith, it acknowledged God's gifts to her, His glorious designs for her, and His work in her, with as frank a simplicity as her own "low estate;" she could sing as well as "ponder;" she received the exceeding honour as meekly as the poverty; and among the many blessings which united to weave the crown of beatitude which is hers to all generations, the best of all is, "Blessed is she that *believed.*"

Throughout the scattered notices given of her we may trace the same character. Of the worship paid to the Holy One born of her, by magi and shepherds, and the prophecies concerning Him uttered by Simeon and Anna, we are not told she said anything; but only that she pondered these sayings in her heart. In that lowly, silent, loving mother's heart, she revolved and weighed and treasured those wondrous things for thirty patient years. And then at Cana, when none else knew Jesus save as "the carpenter's son," she expected miracles from Him. The reply of the Lord was doubtless no rebuke; but in the perfect renunciation of self which it involved, how fully and meekly she acquiesced! She was not to share His mission or His glory, save as his disciple; but His glory, and not her own, was the thing on which her heart was set; and she said to the servants, with calm acquiescence of humility, and joyful self-renunciation of love, "Whatever He saith unto you, do it."

If once the mother's heart overcame the disciple's faith, and she would in a pang of anxiety —remembering perhaps the ominous words of Simeon—have sacrificed His mission to His safety, we never hear that this was repeated; and faithfully, when the most faithful stood afar off or fled, she stood close by the cross, letting the sword pierce as deep as God would have it into that maternal heart He had so filled with joy. Then, with that last message, that last precious acknowledgment that there was indeed something "between her" and her crucified Saviour, she retired to the home of John to ponder these things in her heart, and, after the ascension, to meet as one of the disciples in the upper room, awaiting the promise from on high. Surely the lives of the saints furnish few such examples of self-renouncing love, and happy, genuine humility! Surely we may all, with full hearts, thank God for His grace in her, and rejoice to call her blessed.

The answer of the heart and the will to the Divine assurance, "The Lord is with thee," when really believed, must ever be like Mary's "Behold the handmaid of the Lord." The heart is bowed in love, the will in submission; being made children by adoption, we are made servants by the Father's favour; God's service being so high a thing, that none are consciously employed on it but His children.

Christianity does not so much exalt woman as exalt service; by making of those lowly offices it is the lot of woman to exercise, a work as high as Gabriel's—" doing the pleasure of God"—the Gospel does not emancipate woman, but makes service free.

With this talisman, in a cottage, woman is a minister of God; without it, on a throne, she is a slave.

God has made us dependent. He made Eve, not for herself, but for Adam; and there is absolutely no escape from God's natural laws. If we do not bow beneath them as an easy yoke, they will fetter us as an iron chain. Man living for himself is indeed a rebel against God, and a traitor to his Christ, and quenches thus his highest faculties; but woman, living for herself, is a rebel against her nature, and a traitor to her necessary destiny, and her heart can find no rest.

The romantic, chivalric ideal of woman, which arose side by side with the worship of Mary, if higher than that of the East, was surely far lower than that of ancient Germany, and infinitely beneath that of Judea.

The Book which shows us Sarah kneading the cakes for Abraham's guests, and Rebekah lifting the pitcher of water to the lips of the weary stranger, shows us also Deborah, the mother in Israel, the poet and the heroine, and Esther the deliverer of her people. And of her who "ate not the bread of idleness," and "rose while it was yet night, and laid her hands to the spindle," it is written, "the heart of her husband safely trusteth in her, and her children arise up and call her blessed."

It was a higher lot for women to be the servants of their husbands at home, toiling to weave their garments and prepare their food and then to be their counsellors in perplexity, as with the old Germans, than to be enshrined in the sentimental visions of a knight-errant, and sit embroidering impossible flowers and impracticable battles whilst desponding lovers broke lances for their smiles. The manly honour of those old Goths was worth all the languishing idolatry of troubadours and transfixed squires; one look of cordial understanding from those staunch warriors would have outweighed all the sighs of all the knights and poets who ever broke lance or penned sonnet in honour of their mistresses' eyebrows, because the qualities esteemed were nobler. The esteem of the one contained more true reverence than all the homage of the other; and loftier than all the titles romance or chivalry ever invented, are the names—friend, wife, mother. Worship debases a creature instead of exalting it; it degrades the object worshipped as well as the worshipper. An idol, whether a silver crucifix or a statuette from Pompeii, is little removed from a plaything; and household gods require small transformation to become drawing-room ornaments.

The German ideal, penetrated and illumined by a higher, even that which Jesus said was God's purpose from the beginning, has ended in the homes of Christian Europe, of England and English America. The romantic ideal sank into the courts of Charles II. and Louis XIV. The conventional refinements which tend to deprive woman of work, deprive her also of dignity. To be truly the equal and companion of man, she must be his fellow-worker and his helpmeet. Effeminacy is as far removed from what is truly womanly as from what is truly manly.

But in that expression, "the handmaid of the Lord," much more is implied than mere work. The work must be *service;* and the very commencement and crown of service is *submission.* This sentence, inwardly digested, is the antidote to restless ambition as much as to indolent inactivity. Uttered in the various keys in which the strings it touches are tuned, it may be the calm acquiescence of martyrdom, the childlike language of trust and submission, or the joyful sacrament of allegiance and active service.

It is not work in the abstract we are called upon to undertake; it is not *our* work, but *God's* work. The Church is not left in the world with a certain amount of work to accomplish, of which each may choose his own portion. It is an ordered household. The Master assigns to each as much the daily task as the daily bread. Indeed, so essential is this submission, that in some cases it seems the only task assigned. Of so little importance is the work of our hands in the sight of Him who framed the worlds with a word, the myriads of the heavenly host beholding! In all cases it is the first step—the first act of service required of us. Nothing is more essential for us to remember than that all *work* is not *service,* and all *service* is not *work.*

Let us be very careful of thinking on the one hand that we have no work assigned us to do, or on the other hand that what we have assigned to us is not the right thing for us. If ever we can say in our hearts to God, in reference to any daily duty, "This is not my place; I would choose something dearer; I am capable of something higher;" we are guilty not only of rebellion but of blasphemy. It is equivalent to saying, not only, "My heart revolts against Thy commands," but, "Thy commands are unwise; Thine Almighty guidance is unskillful; Thine Omniscient Eye has mistaken the capacities of Thy creature; Thine infinite love is indifferent to the welfare of Thy child." Awful as this is, this, and no less, is the message which every murmur of our hearts bears to heaven.

But murmurs can only be frozen into silence by commands; God loves best to melt them into gratitude by mercies. If we realized the full dignity and blessedness of the destiny, Handmaid of the Lord! what it is to be permitted to serve God at all, we should scarcely stay to consider what our position in the household might be. It is because we do not rejoice as we might in God's gifts that we do not rejoice as we should in His commands.

Children of God! The words are so familiar that they glide from our lips like a mere conventional title; were the thing as familiar to our inmost hearts we should scarcely utter the words without tears of adoring, wondering gratitude; we should know that angels know no loftier or dearer name. Following this relationship upward into its brightest results of glory, it leads the apostle to anticipations

Hope's furthest gaze fails to fathom. "If children, then heirs, heirs of God, joint-heirs with Christ." Following it earthward, through all its blessed consequences of duty, it brings us first to this—servants, purchased household servants of the Highest—" handmaids of the Lord."

If the relationship of a child introduces us into the highest privilege of angels, the office of a servant makes us partakers of their highest employment. It brings into the most monotonous and ordinary life the aims of the very loftiest: it changes life from an exile or a summer tour into an earnest pilgrimage to a Holy Place, into a happy journey to a blessed Home. God begins our spiritual life by making all things ours; we must commence our service by owning ourselves altogether His.

Not that this submission, this absolute surrendering of self to God, involves a lulling of the will, or of any one faculty, to sleep. The will is not to be cast away, but laid on the altar. Not as "dead corpses," but as "living sacrifices" must we enter the "company of Jesus." Oh that every morning, waking in the presence of God, the salutation which the first ray of recovered light brought to us could be —" Child of God, Handmaid of the Lord, a forgiven and a consecrated being!" What alacrity it would give to our movements, what reality to our communion with God, what earnestness and sweetness to our intercourse with one another. If every morning, if but one morning, the whole multitude of believers, the whole family on earth, would gather round the Father, and each ask, "Lord, what *this day* wouldst Thou have me to do?" as one by one left the Royal Audience, each with a special commission, what a rich day that would be for the Church and the world! What broken hearts would be bound up, what feeble hands would be lifted up, what blind eyes would be opened, how many tears would be wiped away, how many burdens lightened, how many lost souls brought back, how many weary "because of the way" be sent "on their way rejoicing!" So much does God in His sovereignty suffer to depend on human instrumentality.

Jesus does not now send His disciples two and two through the cities and villages, to return to Him after many days; He does not give us a scheme of duty for a year, or a month, or a week. We must wait on His behest morning by morning. To-morrow's duties will certainly be a burden too heavy for us to bear, and yesterday's orders are a forgery, without seal or signature, if we copy them over for to-day. How many blessed messages may we not have already missed by failing thus to wait! Bending over that word of His, which is ever fresh as if it fell from His lips to-day (does it not come fresh from His Spirit to ours to-day?), let us bow our souls and say: "Behold the handmaid of the Lord!" let us lift up our hearts and ask, "Lord, what wouldst Thou have me to do?" Then light from the opened heaven shall stream on our daily task, revealing the grains of gold where yesterday all seemed dust; a Hand shall sustain us and our daily burden, so that, smiling at yesterday's fears, we shall say: *This is easy, this is light;* every "lion in the way," as we come up to it, shall be seen chained, and leave open the gates of the Palace Beautiful; and to us, even to us, feeble and fluctuating as we are, ministeries shall be assigned, and through our hands blessings shall be conveyed, in which the spirits of just men made perfect might delight.

Such ministries must have a countless variety of forms; but the character is for all alike. There is for us, as for the angels, the service of warfare. We are sworn to fight manfully under

His banner against the three enemies—the world, the flesh and the devil; the two first being but the weapons of the last—the visible weapons by which alone we can recognize the hand of the invisible foe; against our evil and selfish self, a war of extermination; against the world, of invasion and conquest; a warfare which can scarcely be distinguished from our ministry, inasmuch as the weapons of our warfare are also the implements of our work.

Is not the commonest and most successful wile of Satan, next to lulling us to sleep, to transfer the field of battle from the sanctuary of God to the darkness of our own hearts? His great aim is to keep us struggling outside the pavilion, in which God secretly hides His beloved, instead of entering within, where the Evil One cannot come. Once at the feet of Jesus, humbly abiding there, the victory is gained, at least the victory in that battle, for the warfare never ceases. The tempter cannot bear the light of those eyes which rest in love on us, or stand one touch of that pierced and victorious hand; at the determinate girding on of the heavenly armour, and facing him in God's strength, he flees. And when, with our armour on—those swords, which are plowshares in the spiritual husbandry, and those spears, which are pruning-hooks in Christ's vineyard*—that panoply of peace, love, joy, faith, humility, which is at once armour, clothing and implements of work—we go about our daily tasks, are we not fighting in the most effective way *as we serve?*

The services appointed us are so various, that it is impossible to indicate them. For some, life is so full of sweet home-duties, every moment comes so laden with its task, the garden is so full of indigenous flowers, each with its store of honey for food, and wax for building, that the question is rather, " What am I to do first ?" than " What am I to do ?" Whilst to others, were there not the family of God in the world, and the grace of God in the heart, no necessary task might seem allotted. Both cases have their blessings and their trials. If we would but each of us gather the flowers in our path as diligently as we sometimes do the thorns, our hands would be more fitted for our work, and our homes more full of fragrance than they are. The richest who count what they have not, are poor, and the poorest who count what they have, are rich. It is sweet when the

* Of course, by *application*, not by *interpretation*.

heart's natural affections are God's appointed taskmaster. It is well, also, when the heart is "at leisure from itself," to pour its whole wealth, and bend its whole energies on the voluntary service of others; when the last commands of the Master to the disciples take the place of the dictates of instinctive affection. In both spheres, the real blessing and the real strength must spring from the full apprehension of the living Fountain of all love, and all authority, and the frequent application to it. The poorest and the richest in God's best earthly gift of natural relationship, are really happy just in the proportion that they believe the truth—"The Lord is with thee;" and useful, just in the proportion that they live "handmaids of the Lord."

But surely none are so full of cares, or so poor in gifts, that to them also, waiting patiently and trustfully on God for His daily commands, He will not give direct ministry for Him, increasing according to their strength and their desire. There is so much to be set right in the world, there are so many to be led, and helped, and comforted, that we must continually come in contact with such in our daily life. Let us only take care, that, by the glance being turned inward, or strained onward, or lost in vacant reverie, we do not miss our turn of service, and pass by those to whom we might have been sent on an errand straight from God.

But all service is not work, at least not outward work. Perhaps we do not think enough what an effective service prayer is, especially intercessory prayer, direct application by name for others, laying their needs and cares—all they would or might request for themselves—before God. We do not believe as we should how it might help those we so fain would serve, penetrating the hearts we cannot open, shielding those we cannot guard, teaching where we cannot speak, comforting where our words have no power to soothe; following the steps of our beloved through the toils and perplexities of the day, lifting off their burdens with an unseen hand at night. No ministry is so like that of an angel's as this—silent, invisible, known but to God; through us descends the blessing, and to Him alone ascends the thanksgiving. Surely not an employment brings us so near to God and the spirits of men as intercessory prayer. There is a depth of wisdom in the words, "If we only spoke more to God for man than even to man for God!"

Of the other secret service, thanksgiving—the "service of song" in the heart—the more of it there is, the more the heart will glow inwardly, and the life shine outwardly. We know what reason there is for thanksgiving. The one theme of pardon might fill eternity, and pardon is but the first in an endless series of blessings. Every day brings them in multitudes: and above all, every day opens our eyes to the unspeakable gift which sweetens and hallows and transcends them all.

It is said, that if you connect a room in which an orchestra is playing, by a metallic rod, with the sounding-board of a harp in a remote apartment of the same building, " by placing the ear close to the instrument a diminutive band is heard, in which all the instruments preserve their distinctive qualities, and the pianos and fortes, crescendos and diminuendos, their relative contrasts. Compared with an ordinary band heard at a distance through the air, the effect is as of a landscape seen in miniature beauty through a concave lens, compared with the same scene viewed by ordinary vision through a murky atmosphere." Is it not thus with the thankful heart, the heart brought by faith and love into connection with heaven?

The songs of the multitude there vibrate through the sympathetic strings, and those who come near, not knowing perchance the cause, yet hear the music, and learning first to love the echo, may ere long learn to love and join the song; whilst to those faint vibrations He, in whose praise heaven itself is filled with perpetual song, listens and rejoices; "for with such sacrifices God is well pleased."

Such are our aims: how far, far below them our attainments. We may not lower our ideal; yet when we compare our attempts at attaining it with the perfect example—an example far more perfect than that of Mary, even of Him who pleased not Himself, and came not to be ministered unto, but to minister—we may well weep, and we might well despair, were not the example also the sacrifice, His righteousness ours to justify as well as to imitate—did not His precious blood atone for the iniquity of our holy things, cleansing not only our original guilt, but our daily defilement—had not He himself engaged one day to perfect in us our marred and feeble copies—were not He himself our propitiation and our advocate—His will our sanctification—His promise, that when we see Him as He is, we shall serve Him day and night, "without spot or wrinkle, or any such thing," transformed into His own perfect image.

Then, of the rewards of service. If, during the period which succeeds the Resurrection of Life and precedes the Resurrection of Judgment, rewards may be assigned proportioned to the services rendered here, blessed are those who receive them. Heavenly crowns are placed on the head of man only that they may be cast at the feet of Christ. The amount of service in glory may be increased by the amount of service in suffering here; the cities reigned over may be proportioned to the talents used, and those who have exercised most loving ministries on earth, may, when the heavens are opened, and the angels of God ascend and descend upon the Son of man, and the children of the resurrection are like the angels, be oftenest sent on errands of blessing to that earth over which the Crucified shall reign. The service on earth will thus be rewarded by fuller power of service in heaven, and the rule of the Church militant, "He that would be great among you let him be your minister, and he that would rule as he that doth serve," become the joy of the Church triumphant.

The sentences of the world may then be

strangely reversed : services rewarded now with acclamations may then be scarcely remembered by Him who valued the widow's farthing above all the overflowings of abundance ; and many who toil unnoticed here may there be among the chief princes. Could we see things in the light of that day, we might find our ambitions run altogether in a contrary direction. Hidden paths of humble service, or costly sacrifice, or noiseless conflict, might be coveted with a zeal as eager and as selfish as now the highest place of rule and honour. But this cannot be ; heaven's crowns will be placed on the heads of those who least expect them.

Yet the highest reward and the highest motive must ever be the same. The love of Christ is the constraining power to His service on earth ; the love of Christ is the joy of the marriage-supper in heaven, and blessed are they who are called to it—called to it by free unmerited love, arrayed for it in no garb of human weaving or earthly dye, but with robes washed and made white in the blood of the Lamb. The "best robe" is that common to all ; the priestly garments made white "as no fuller on earth can white them" in the atoning blood of Jesus.

THE FRIENDSHIP OF THE COUSINS.

Luke i. 43–55.

Elizabeth said, Whence is this to me, that the mother of my Lord should come to me?

And Mary said, My soul doth magnify the Lord, and my spirit hath rejoiced in God my Saviour. For he hath regarded the low estate of his handmaiden: for, behold, from henceforth all generations shall called me blessed. For He that is mighty hath done to me great things; and holy is his name. And his mercy is on them that fear him from generation to generation. He hath shewed strength with his arm; he hath scattered the proud in the imagination of their hearts. He hath put down the mighty from their seats, and exalted them of low degree. He hath filled the hungry with good things; and the rich he hath sent empty away. He hath holpen his servant Israel, in remembrance of his mercy; as he spake to our fathers, to Abraham, and to his seed for ever.

IV.

THE FRIENDSHIP OF THE COUSINS.

IF the pictures the Bible gives us of heaven prove to us they are drawn by a hand within the veil, it is no less so with its biographies. Unlike all other histories, it is the history of homes; it records not merely the movement of the hands, but the secret of the hidden springs. Its characters are drawn by a hand which can touch the inmost depths of the heart; its biographies are written by One who dwells *within* the home.

The interview with the angel was over. Gabriel departed from Mary, and with that wondrous hope in her heart which was to transform her quiet home in Galilee into the shrine of her God, and make her lowly history the turning-point in the history of the world, she arose "with haste," and went to the hill-country to her cousin Elizabeth. Were there none among her kindred in Nazareth to whom Mary could open her heart? Gentle and retiring we know her nature was, given to pondering in the heart more than to much speaking; and it is very probable that those who, after thirty years' acquaintance with Jesus in His home, and three years' watching of His miracles and His teaching—miracles which healed and fed thousands, and teaching which silenced Sadducees and Pharisees, yet believed not on Him —would have regarded the narrative of her angelic vision as the idle dream of an enthusiastic girl: "What will this dreamer say?"

She had indeed, we know, one sister, the wife of Cleophas, the mother of James the Less and Joses—a sister, or perhaps a cousin as dear, one of whom it is never said, "she believed not," who stood with Mary at the cross, and did what it seems Mary could not do, came early to the sepulchre. But of the rest of her Galilean relations, we have no record during those three and thirty years but words of insulting unbelief in Jesus. The hearts that could coldly carp at Him, had scarcely received reverently the intimation of Gabriel's visit. Not that the brethren of the Lord must necessarily have been men of peculiar incredulity and heartlessness. After the Resurrection, before the three thousand had been added to the Church, when to Israel in general the last sight of Jesus had been on the cross, their hearts were melted, and those who had doubted their kinsman, Jesus of Nazareth, abode in the upper room with the apostles, and with Mary, and waited in prayer and supplication for the promise of their ascended Lord. But they were cautious. The claims advanced, if not true, were so tremendous; and as they returned from the day's labours in the corn-fields on the plain, or from pruning the olives and vines on the hills, or sate buying and selling, and working with their hands, in the streets of their little town, what traces could they see that an angel had been there? No star abode over the house of Mary; no glory played around her head. It was very true, that more than two thousand years ago angels had appeared to Abraham, and wonderful things were read sometimes on the Sabbath-days in the synagogues, of what Isaiah and Daniel had seen; but that was in the Scriptural times, and they did not live in Scriptural times! The last prophet had died four hundred years since, and no one they knew had heard of such a thing as an angel coming down with a message from God. It was true, also, that the Messiah was yet to come, the son of David, the King of Israel; but what had that to do with them—poor, humble folk at Nazareth? The prophets said nothing about Nazareth. Even at Jerusalem, when they went up to the feast, the doctors scarcely knew of the existence of the place—it must be explained—" Nazareth, a city of Galilee;" their provincial Galileanisms were a jest to the refined tongues of the metropolis; and although they knew their city gleamed afar from its hill-top over the fertile valley, still they could not pretend that there was any thing sacred in the name : " Search, and look, for out of Galilee ariseth no prophet." " Can any good thing come out of Nazareth ?" It was also true that some of them were of the house and lineage of David; but so, probably, were a hundred other families, and no one thought of inquiring in those days about old Hebrew pedigrees, except when it was a case of taxing. The Idumæan sat on the throne of Israel; the Roman ruled in Jerusalem. Royal connexions are not ordinarily of much avail in the fortieth generation; and many a descendant of Plantagenets and Hohenstaufen, may now be plowing or watchmaking, with as little thought of the British or Austrian thrones, as the kinsmen of Mary of the throne of David. Not that pedigrees can be to any modern nation of the same importance as the Great Promise made them to the Jews; the genealogies even of peasants of that royal line were, we know, carefully kept; but when it came to the actual fulfillment of such a promise, how could any eyes, unillumined by prayer and faith, see in their kinswoman, the wife of the carpenter, or in Him they knew as the " carpenter's son," the mother all generations shall call blessed, and the Christ of God?

To learn the moral of these ancient histories, it is essential that we bring the characters down from the mountain-mists of centuries to the every-day standard and the every-day atmosphere of our own times.

We cannot then wonder that Mary hastened with her hidden hope away from Nazareth, to the home of Elizabeth.

The angel had departed from Mary, but the Lord was with her; with her in the long and difficult journey over the hills of Galilee, not then hallowed with New Testament associations (for the first page of the New Testament history was then beginning to be lived)—perhaps through that royal city over which the Holy One to be born of her was to reign, by Bethlehem, the city of David, through the plain of Mamre, where Abraham pitched his tent—to Hebron, the priestly city, the city of refuge, among the hills. The Lord was with her; and she trusted in Him; never, therefore, could she have wanted companionship and help; yet the human heart yearned for human companionship and sympathy, and He who knows it must ever be thus, had added to the angel's message to herself tidings about her cousin Elizabeth. The angel who announced to her her glorious destiny, had also introduced her to a friend—the one who, in all the world, could best have understood and communed with her. Bound together by similar hopes, the mother of the prophet and the mother of the Lord were made known to one another by the lips of an angel, by God himself. Is not the lesson to be drawn from this inexpressibly sweet? His presence, His all-sufficiency, are not the substitute for all other blessings, but the source of all. The Father is not jealous of the friendships of His children; He forms them, He creates the spiritual relationship in the heart, and then he binds the hearts together. When the Bible tells us God is a jealous God, it does not mean that the affections must be cramped and pruned lest they grow too luxuriantly; it does not mean that we need fear to love those He has given us too much. There is no intensity of pure human love, no overflowing of natural affection, in which He does not rejoice; He has "*so* loved us." It means simply, that, if we make idols of His gifts, forgetting Him in them, He knows they cease to be blessings. The aqueduct broken from the spring can convey no living water; if we do not love Him with the whole heart, the heart must contract; and He loves us too truly, is, indeed, too jealous of our love and happiness, to suffer this. But in Him there cannot be a tie too strong, or an affection too intense. The angel who told Mary that the Lord was with her, led her to the friendship of Elizabeth. Is it not a happiness to dwell on the thought of what that intercourse must have been? what mutual rejoicing, what delight in the seal each would see shining on each other's brow! At the first salutation of Mary, what joy and humility in Elizabeth! The first words of Mary are a song—a song which has throbbed through the heart of the Church for eighteen centuries. "What is this that the mother of my Lord should come to me? And Mary said, "My soul doth magnify the Lord, and my spirit hath rejoiced in God my Saviour.

The first greeting is all that is told us of the intercourse of the three months; but what a key it is! We do not know if the cousins had ever met before; if at any of those annual feasts at Jerusalem, which must have been such family gatherings, the eye of the childless Elizabeth had rested fondly on the face of the young maiden from Galilee; if Mary had ever cheered that blameless aged woman, the priest's wife, with little acts of filial kindness. Fancy may dwell fondly on such pictures, and the angel's "Thy cousin Elizabeth" has something of a familiar sound, but from Bible history, faith draws more touching portraits.

Elizabeth and Zacharias were old. Many long years had passed since the Hebrew priest had taken to his home, in the old Levitical city, the daughter of the house of Aaron—long years of hope deferred. Other homes, more recent echoed with the laughter, and the sweet earnestness of childish voices. Other hearts expanded with those far-reaching hopes which made the future tangible: to them, no such sweet cares and serious joys were given. To them, the present brought no happy throng of loving toils and duties, and the future was but the repetition of to-day. Youth passed with its fluctuations of hope and fear ; middle age came with its sober autumnal gray, brightened for them by no sweet second spring-time of new life blooming in its midst.

Zacharias prayed, prayers for the faithful Israelite sustained by many a promise ; but they seemed to fall heavily from the impenetrable walls of heaven, bringing back nothing but their echo. Gradually, the fervent longing subsided into the settled sorrow, " the Child" being not yet " born," " the Son" not yet " given," to expectant Israel and to the lost world. Yet, during all these years, they " walked in all the commandments and ordinances of the Lord blameless ;" blameless, then, of embittering God's chastening by murmurs or distrust. And, doubtless, to these blameless ones the ordinances of their God brought many a joy unasked. The commandments of the Old Testament are not all negative ; and " blameless" in the sight of God, must mean far more than " harmless." The fatherless could not be relieved without relieving the heart of the childless; the "heavy burdens" they helped to bear must have lightened their own; from the hungry "they fed," refreshment came back to them; the widow they "pleaded for," pleaded to God for them; and the home to which "the poor were brought," and where the "outcast" found a refuge, could have been no desolate place. Doubtless, also, God sent them many a sweet natural pleasure. He has many vintages from which to fill the cup, and often makes it run over with living water from the rock. But they were old; and when, according to the custom of the priests' office, Zacharias went up once more to Jerusalem, heavily must the sound of the farewell have fallen on Elizabeth, for "reproach" had sunk into her heart, and it left her in her old age, alone. The unanswered prayers of earlier days were long since forgotten.

Forgotten by Zacharias, but not by God! Through those long years of trial He had watched His children, treasuring in His hands for them the very joy they desired; and at eventide, when the gardens and vineyards of life, its rich valleys and sunny plains, lay far behind, and up the solitary mountain they toiled, waiting only for the prospect on the other side —there, in the desert, He had prepared for them a fountain of joy and gladness—a joy which His eye had seen all the while, and to which their weary steps had all the while been drawing nearer.

In every trial, of every kind, for every one of us, is it not the same? The answer may come sooner or later; the well of joy for which the heart yearns may be opened early in the pilgrimage, or not till near the mountain-top; or it may not flow for us until we reach the other side; but surely, unfailingly, we are drawing near the answer to all our prayers. God never gives less than we ask, and often gives a hundredfold. He sees the moment which shall change our mourning into dancing. In His hand are stored the very blessings that we need; and the rich harvest of many a forgotten prayer shall yet clothe our hearts, until they stand so thick with unexpected blessing that they "laugh and sing." "*Thy prayer is heard, and thou shalt have joy and gladness.*" This is the unfailing message awaiting all who pray.

Such experiences had Elizabeth to unfold to Mary, to her on whose lowly head had descended, unsought, a promise beyond all human request.

Happy friendships are those between the young and the old, endeared to the one by the sweet early associations that they recall, and to the other by all the tenderness of ties which must before very long be severed; the natural freshness of youth breathing like a mountain breeze on the heart of the aged, and the rich experience of age poured into the heart of youth. Blessed indeed, when on the one side on the roses of earth rest the dews of heaven; and on the other, the experience of life has been not only of hopes decayed and sorrows endured, but of sorrows hallowed, and of a Hope every faltering footstep brings nearer; when years of conscious weakness and "sufficient" grace have added depth to sympathy, and tenderness to pity; when in the matured graces of "such an one as Paul the aged," we see the blessed possibility of keeping the affections unspotted from the world and undimmed by time, and through the fading form can catch the glow and the earnest joyousness of that eternal youth, in which after ages of angelic life the "young men in shining garments" watched by the opened sepulchre of the Lord.

Rich memories of olden days floated around the home of Zacharias and Elizabeth. In the vineyards, on those terraced hills, hung the heavy purple clusters of the grapes of Eshcol. From that height Caleb drove the giant race of the Anakims—the old man, whose strength at fourscore and five was fresh for war, both to go out and come in, as when at forty Moses sent him to spy out the land, and he spoke with such a noble trust in God amidst the unbelieving host. In the fields around lay the upper and nether springs which the old hero's bounty added to the dowry of his daughter. In those plains at the mountain's foot, Abraham had pitched his tent, and the Lord had appeared to him. Under the broad shadow of that terebinth-tree, Hebrew legend said the three heavenly guests had rested themselves awhile, whilst Sarah made cakes on the hearth within the tent, of the three measures of fine meal, and the calf tender and good was fetched from the herd grazing around. On the road leading eastward toward the cities of the plain, where now the Dead Sea heaved, Abraham had pleaded with God for Sodom. Thither David went up by God's command, and there he dwelt, "waxing stronger and stronger, whilst the house of Saul waxed weaker and weaker," until all the elders of Israel came up thither to him, and the secret anointing of Samuel was at length recognized by the whole nation, and there they anointed David king.

Hebron was also a city of the priests. There were the home of many who during the time of their ministrations dwelt in the upper chambers of the temple, who bathed in its sacred lavers, and trod its courts as their abode—who sacrificed the morning and evening sacrifices, and offered the perpetual incense on the golden altar—and ate of the sacred bread, and filled the bowls of the golden candlestick with holy oil, and watched it burning through the silent night, throwing the light from its golden almond-branches on the purple folds of the vail with its embroidery of cherubim.

And, alas! what narratives of riot and covetousness and profanation must Zacharias have brought back from the holy city, to mar those sacred associations! " Righteousness lodged in her, but now murderers."

Hebron was also a city of refuge. Along the " broad roads" which mercy had provided, had pressed the eager feet of many a fugitive fleeing from the avenger of blood ; and, the steep sides of that hill once scaled, within those walls many a trembling heart had felt the grateful glow of safety. With such memories and such hopes—local legend giving life to the records of Scriptural history—amid such scenes passed the three months of intercourse between the cousins: and though to them old Nineveh lay buried among its sand-heads, and the earth was a square building on pillars, and the sky a concave roof hung with a great many lamps, and not a book probably was known except the rolls of the law and the prophets carefully stored in the synagogue, conversation could never have lacked interest. For though their visible world was much narrower than ours, angels dwelt in it, and the living God reigned in it, and they, the daughters of Israel, were immortal. Poorer though their past was by eighteen centuries and by the whole New Testament, and narrow as their present sphere might seem, their future was as infinite as ours.

And in that future, linked to their own lowly lives, were the names of the "greatest born of women" and of Jesus. In all that song, that inspired hymn of the virgin, two elements are conspicuous; two interwoven melodies make all its music. Self abased, God exalted: in self, humiliation; in God her Saviour, joy: Mary of low estate, of low degree, among the poor and hungry; God, He who is mighty, doing great things to her, He, whose name is holy, whose mercy is from generation to generation on them that fear Him, who hath showed strength with His arm, who hath exalted them of low degree, and filled the hungry with good things. The hymn bears on its brow the seal of the beatitude of her who sang it. "Blessed are the poor in spirit, for theirs is the kingdom of heaven."

According to the just proportion of these two elements is all the blessedness of our intercourse with one another now. If God is exalted, we are united; if self is exalted, in ever so slight a degree, whether by self-love or by that morbid self-depreciation which is but self-esteem wounded, in that degree we come within one another's atmosphere of repulsion, and can know no true communion. In the low place, all the waters of love, the dew from heaven, and the springs of earth, flow naturally into the heart. Happily for us, the first step is not to empty but to fill; the heart *cannot* empty itself; we can no more displace selfishness from our hearts by laborious efforts at self-renunciation, than we can expel stagnant water from a pond by stirring it. The fresh streams of God's love must flow into the heart, and they will purify as well as fill it. Any fresh stream of love may do this for a time, but the love of God only for ever, because it alone is ever pure, unintermittent and inexhaustible.

The *first* words of our psalm of life must ever be, "My soul doth magnify the Lord, and my spirit hath rejoiced in God my Saviour."

THE HOME AT NAZARETH.

Luke ii. 51, 52.

And he went down with them, and came to Nazareth, and was subject unto them: but his mother kept all these sayings in her heart. And Jesus increased in wisdom and stature, and in favour with God and man.

V.

THE HOME AT NAZARETH.

WE, who are often so impatient if our work is not assigned the moment the desire for it is awakened, and if we cannot see, or, like the man in the German tale with the wonderful hearing, almost *hear* our purposes grow into fruit—how much do we need to learn from this history!

Thirty years Mary waited for the fulfillment of the promises concerning her Son, and then the fulfillment commenced by His baptism amongst the publicans and sinners who sought the son of Elizabeth, and by the temptation in the wilderness. Thirty years the Son of God abode in silence on earth, with no manifestation of His divine origin, and no commencement of His divine mission. During the whole of those thirty years, the records concerning Him would scarcely fill a page of our New Testaments.

Why this long silence of the lips which, at twelve years old, could have refuted all the false teachers, and satisfied all the eager inquirers in the world? False prophets were going about, error was being diligently sown all around Him, and all around Him He who knew what was in man saw minds gasping for light, and hearts hungering for spiritual food; and yet He, the light of the world, was in it and continued hidden. He who knew the answer to every sophism which can bewilder the intellect, and the solution of every problem which can agitate the heart, remained silent, going in and out among those He came to save, and seeing them sin and err—yet, until the word from His Father came, going in and out amongst them only (as they supposed) as the "carpenter's son." The mystery of those thirty years of patient silence we cannot fathom; their lesson of obedience, and self-renunciation, and entire yielding up of the will to God, we cannot bind too close around our hearts.

One pearl at least we may draw up from the depths of those long, silent years. He who could not but be always about His Father's business, was proving all the while the sacredness of human relationships in the sight of God.

At the very dawning of His earthly life it was not so. "Heaven" did, indeed, "lie visibly about" Him in His "infancy;" angels gathered in multitudes, and the heavenly hosts sang heavenly hymns on the hills of Bethlehem, when Christ the Lord lay in the manger there; they hovered around His infant slumbers. The shepherds returned glorifying and praising God, when they had seen the babe wrapped in swaddling clothes; and all they that heard it, wondered at those things that were told them by the shepherds. The Magi came from the East, led by the star, and perhaps by the light of some old prophecy—relics of the captivity of Jewish prophets—to worship Him who was born King of the Jews. The star abode over where the young child was; the poverty of the dwelling could not veil from their adoring eyes that it was a palace; and the destitution of His infancy was relieved by gifts offered as if to a king. Gold shone in the manger, and incense perfumed it, and myrrh, if it witnessed of the death He came to suffer, spoke also of a royal embalming. When the Magi had departed, an angel came in the night, and warned Joseph of the danger which threatened that sacred life. In the temple, also, the Spirit of God gathered those who looked for redemption in Israel around the babe; and the lowly offering which the merciful law appointed, that the poorest parents might not come emptyhanded before God, the pair of turtle-doves, could not conceal from Simeon and Anna, that the first-born of the Galilean peasant was indeed, not only holy to the Lord, but the Holy One of God. Again, sacred songs attended the path of the Saviour, and a Psalm, inspired by the Holy Ghost, sounded through the temple to greet the Son of David; and Mary heard of her infant as she gave Him into the arms of the old man, that He was "the salvation of God, the light of the Gentiles, the glory of Israel;" and that the joy of beholding Him was such, that afterwards, nothing seemed left for Simeon but to "depart in peace."

But after that, all relapsed into silence. "The angels went away into heaven," and Joseph and Mary were left to flee by night (whether by sea, or through the desert) into Egypt, carrying with them as a helpless babe, the Saviour of the world, fleeing from death, as if the enemy could have touched Him ere He chose, bearing no sign of royalty but the hatred of King Herod. We are not told that any miraculous fountains were opened for these fugitives in the desert, or that they were fed with bread from heaven. They probably knew what it was to seek employment from the rich Jews of Egypt (perhaps amongst the Jewish colony of Alexandria), and to eat the bread of the stranger. Jesus also, like Israel of old, was to be a stranger in the land of Egypt. Thence, indeed, God "called His Son." When the danger was over, once more an angel appeared to Joseph in a dream, and they returned to Nazareth: and thenceforth, marked by no distinction of honor or danger, of friendship from heaven or of enmity from hell, the even tenor of their monotonous life of labor went on for many years unbroken, save by one incident.

Every year, that poor, but faithful Hebrew family went up to Jerusalem to keep the Passover; the one annual event in their laborious and even life. Of the converse which then took place, how those who waited for redemption in Israel gathered around the Holy Child, and rejoiced to see Him "waxing strong in spirit, filled with wisdom, and with the grace of God," we are not told. Many changes must have been witnessed by those annual gatherings; those milestones along the way of life. If

Joseph and Mary came from Galilee to the feast of their God, Zacharias and Elizabeth would surely come from Hebron; and that group, over which Christian art has so lovingly brooded, may actually have been gathered in Jerusalem. The virgin mother, with the child Jesus, really a child, a "young child," helpless and dependent, with the smile of a child's love and gladness on His lips and in His eyes: the other child of promise, from the desert, where, till his showing forth unto Israel, he abode—clad, it may be, in the prophetic garb, with the shadow of his early ministry and martyrdom on His brow—and bending over the three with matronly tenderness, instead of the traditional St. Anne, Elizabeth, the cousin of Mary, rejoicing in her son, and in her Saviour.

These scenes may have been witnessed in Jerusalem: and around that Holy Family what converse must have been held, and what prayers offered, could the air but yield up its hidden stores of scenes and sounds. But God has not caused that picture to be drawn for us, nor those words to be recorded; and we are left to imagine, how, one by one, the band of aged saints entered into their rest; how one year Zacharias was missed from his priestly ministrations, and before another, Elizabeth lay buried in Hebron, leaving the child of their old age to be trained of God in the wilderness, and the home in the hill-country passed away, and none were left to share with Mary the memory of those three months—and Anna, the prophetess, entered into the Temple above, to serve God there day and night, and never go out thence—and Simeon departed in peace.

One only of those annual visits is narrated: when the child Jesus, missed among the returning pilgrims, and sought for sorrowing, was found in His Father's house, about His business —in the temple, in the midst of the doctors, both hearing them, and asking them questions. What thoughts those questions awakened, or what perplexities His answers solved, we know not. We are only told that all who heard Him marvelled; that Joseph and Mary had become so accustomed to beholding Him during those twelve years, as the child in the home, that even to Mary the intimation of His dignity and His mission was a saying not to be understood; and, that after that brief anticipation of His ministry, and from that attentive audience of the Rabbis in the temple, He went back with Mary and her husband to Nazareth, and " was subject to them." Of the eighteen following years we have no record, save of Mary pondering these things, and keeping these sayings in her heart, and Jesus being "subject," and increasing in wisdom, and stature, and in favour with God and man.

We cannot penetrate that silence. It is the silence itself which is our deepest teacher. Yet how sometimes the heart yearns for one more glimpse of what the child Jesus was—for one fragment of those many conversations about the home at Nazareth which must have passed between the mother of Jesus and the beloved disciple, when he took her from the cross to his own home. But not one is given.

We can only conjecture, from the cessation of the mention of the name of Joseph at the marriage of Cana, when "the mother of Jesus was there;" and again, when afterwards Jesus went down to Capernaum, "He and His mother and His brethren," that the "just man" who had so tenderly watched over the infancy of the Saviour was no more, and that Mary was widowed.

It seems also that no son was given to Mary, the wife of Joseph; or, at least, that the crucifixion left her childless and a widow, or she would scarcely have been committed by Him who held human relationships so sacred, as a dying legacy to John. "The only son of his mother, and she was a widow," may have had a prophetic sound of peculiar tenderness to Him who had compassion on her, and touched the bier.*

And from the envious reproach of His fellow-townsmen we glean, wonderful as the thought is, that the Lord was known to them not only as the carpenter's son, but as "the carpenter;" that He actually worked with His hands, labored for daily bread; bearing also in His sinless humanity that portion of the original sentence on fallen man. It may be that He who had stooped to the dependence of infancy, stood also to toil for her who bore Him, and that the widowed Mary had to depend on the labors of His hands—those hands which fed five thousand with five loaves, but never wrought a miracle, nor were lifted up in prayer, to exempt Himself from hunger or from toil. We are sure no rabbinical "Corban" would have freed Him from the bonds of divine law or

---

* A careful comparison of passages seems to show, that those spoken of as the "brethren of the Lord" were the sons of Mary, the wife of Cleophas.

human affection. From Him the command, "Honour thy father and thy mother," came with a force the thunders of Sinai could never give it, the persuasion of human lips, the lips of Him who was subject to His mother: "Who, being in the form of God, thought it not robbery to be equal with God, but made Himself of no reputation, and took on Him the form of a servant."

There is, perhaps, no subject we should approach with such a prayerful reverence as the humanity of our Lord. But this reverence is not cherished by a confusion of the divine and the human: "One altogether; not by confusion of Substance, but by unity of Person." The nearer we approach in the reality of faith to that mystery, the more wonderful it grows. Men at a distance from God and from Christ, may mingle His name with their common conversation, and Christians may make it the subject of theological dispute; but *really near*, the seraphim cover their faces with their wings, and the band of armed men go backwards and fall to the ground. It is remarkable that the disciple whom Jesus loved, who leaned on His breast, who dwelt with His mother, is the one whose writings are the most penetrated with the majesty of His deity.

The very heaven of heavens was not a more sacred place than the home at Nazareth when Jesus was there.

Yet we cannot feel too deeply His real humanity; and in nothing, not even in His hunger in the wilderness, His weariness at Jacob's well, His death even on the cross, does that humanity come so awfully close to us as in the thought of His childhood, and His life in the Galilean home. His infancy even is scarcely so wonderful, though Christian rhetoric has drawn its most striking contrasts thence; and that He who bore up the pillars of the earth should, as a helpless babe, be borne in the arms of a mortal mother, is indeed a depth of condescension.

But that the Christ of God was once actually a child, a child in Mary's home; that *He grew* not merely in stature, but in *wisdom;* that the Truth and the Wisdom of God actually *learned;* that His mind expanded and His affections strengthened—this is surely the deepest wonder of all, because the union of the Godhead with a human soul must ever be a greater mystery than the indwelling of the Godhead in a human body.

Yet so it was. For thirty years, He who

afterwards had not where to lay His head, knew what it was to have a home—knew the tenderness of maternal love. One glimpse into that home is not vouchsafed us ; *but it existed:* and as each day brought a riper beauty to that perfect character, the smile of God rested on Him with ever-increasing complacency, and men loved Him : " He *increased* in *wisdom* and stature, and in *favour with God* and man."

No book of the law could have been possessed in that lowly dwelling. On the Sabbath-day, "as His custom was," He doubtless went into the synagogue, and where, when the hour came, He taught, so that all men wondered, He must often have listened—listened to prophecies of which He was the object and fulfillment, and been silent. But, day by day His " ear was opened" to the Highest teaching ; in God's law did that Blessed One " meditate day and night ;" and He could indeed say, " Thy law is within my heart."

And Mary watched all this ; daily she saw the Spirit waxing strong, and dwelt with Him who loved God perfectly : from whose lips not one light or harsh word ever issued ; in whose sinless soul every grace of the Spirit—love, joy, peace, gentleness, goodness, faith, meekness, temperance—abode, not in conflict, but in an undisputed home: whose delight it was to do all that to fallen man is so difficult, and in whose pure human heart she held a mother's place.

Did Mary know the fullness of the blessing which was hers? Could the overpowering sense that her son was indeed God her Saviour, have been ever with her? It is said that neither she nor Joseph understood Him, when he said, He must be about His Father's business. Human nature is weak, and even with the aid of visible presence, incapable of dwelling ever in the highest communion. Yet, at Cana, she seems to have felt no surprise at His miraculous power. To her it seems to have been a familiar truth; and to her faith, it was enough, without hesitation or repetition, simply to lay the want before Him. "And when they wanted wine, the mother of Jesus said unto Him, They have no wine." Let us not detract from her blessedness. We speak of Eden upon earth, homes of love and peace, scenes of exuberant beauty; but, if ever Eden was restored on earth, it was in that Galilean home of poverty and toil; for there the second Adam dwelt, the Lord from heaven; there the "despised and rejected of men" was "in favour with men;" there the Man of sorrows rested in the favour of God.

Yet, during those thirty years, there were hours, there must have been communion, of which Mary could have known as little as we can; communion between the Son and the Father; prayers within those lowly walls, and on those mountains which girded in the little city; pleadings and sorrows of the Holy One and the Redeemer, which no human thought can comprehend. Mournfully, indeed, must the groans of the marred creation have fallen on the ear of the Creator. Bitterly, in the midst of the favour of men, must the cry, "Crucify Him, crucify Him," have rung on His heart; heavily must the sins of man have pressed on Him, whose inmost soul was perfectly holy—the sins for which He was to be "forsaken" and accursed. No dwelling-place on this fallen earth could have been a resting-place for Him who came from Heaven. Never in this sinful world could the Holy One of God have been other than a man of sorrows. Dwelling from eternity in cloudless joy, Himself the fountain of eternal joy, what could our world have offered Him? Joy, indeed, was before Him—

the divine joy of redeeming; but how was He straitened till this was accomplished! Nevertheless, to Him all nature must have been an open parable; olives, vines and corn-fields, cedars and wild flowers on the hills, the morning songs of birds, the stillness of evening, night with its silent revelations of other worlds, brought Him far more than food, and fragrance and music. He, himself, in the home, on the lonely hill, in the streets of Nazareth, by the shores of Gennesareth—He, and not the marble building on Moriah, with its gilded roofs, was the Temple of God.

That home, that holy subjection of Jesus teaches its own lesson. It is not a mysterious paradise between earth and heaven, but a real home, the model of all others. There is not a home its memory may not hallow, nor a domestic tie it does not consecrate: for it shows what human relationships are in the sight of God; and its images what human relationships may be between renewed hearts. We have so many extremes against which to guard! There is as much danger from superhuman spiritualism, as from ungodly earthliness. Spirituality is opposed, not to humanity, but to worldliness; Jesus, as the Son of man, was not *superhuman*, but sinless and a "*perfect Man.*" His character was not the superseding of humanity, but its perfect development.

And we also, although strangers and pilgrims, have homes on earth. It is by fulfilling, not by surpassing human relationships, we best do His will, and follow Him. Not solitary, but in loving groups, groups God himself has formed, we tread the pathway to heaven. It is not only by being missionaries at home or abroad, but by being as the child, the sister, the wife, the mother, all that the purest natural affections in all these relations can prompt, that we glorify our Father in heaven. The natural affections of the disciples of Jesus, ought to be the strongest and tenderest on earth. A religion which does not draw closer every human tie, bears little impress of Him who had a home at Nazareth, and could care for the welfare of His mother in the agony of redeeming a lost world, saying, " Behold thy mother!" in the same hour that He cried, " My God, my God, why hast Thou forsaken me?"

Let us count up our treasures of kindred; they are our best. Let us "consider" them in the presence of our Father in heaven. Is there any tie which absence has loosened, or which the wear and tear of every-day intercourse, little uncongenialities, unconfessed misunderstandings, have fretted into the heart, until it bears something of the nature of a fetter? Any relationship we have not fully realized for want of dwelling on it? Any cup at our home-table whose sweetness we have not fully tasted, though it might yet make of our daily bread a continual feast? Let us reckon up these treasures now whilst they are still ours, in thankfulness to God. Let us not first learn how large a space of the heart they fill, and might fill with grateful joy, by finding how large a space they have left empty. Let us extend the circle of our relationships wide; *beyond* the home, to those ties of kindred, so close when strengthened by early association, which united Mary and Elizabeth; *within* the home, to those whose connection with us God regards as no loose mechanical bond, but as one of His appointed relationships, placing servants and masters in the next ring of the circle to parents and children. For there is one feature in all human relationships on which we can none of us bear to dwell, yet, if we could let the heart gaze on for a moment, whilst they are yet ours, we might give ourselves and others much more joy, and spare ourselves much of life's very bitterest sorrow—the thought of what might have been. They cannot last for ever. One by one they must be severed; and at last, we must be severed from them all.

Tightly, tenderly, let us bind these blessed ties around our hearts. Let not their strength be first felt as they are broken; let not our first conscious clinging to our beloved, be the convulsive clinging of those who must part. Now, now, let us learn the full worth of our human relationships, counting over, as the veriest misers, the full amount of this our best wealth, that we may use it and enjoy it richly as God would have us.

For we are disciples, not of Him who was in the wilderness until the day of His showing unto Israel, but of Him, who before His ministry as the Christ of God began, dwelt for thirty years with His mother in the home of Nazareth; who has given us as the deepest name of heaven, "My Father's House," and as the dearest title of the Church, the Family of

MARY AMONG THE DISCIPLES.

Matthew xii. 49.

And He stretched forth his hand toward his disciples, and said, Behold my mother and my brethren.

Acts i. 14.

These all continued with one accord in prayer and supplication, with the women, and Mary the mother of Jesus, and with his brethren.

VI.

MARY AMONG THE DISCIPLES.

THE home at Nazareth seems to have been broken up immediately after the "beginning of miracles" in Cana. Yet Mary does not appear to have been separated from Jesus. It is written, that "He, His mother, and His brethren, went down to Capernaum; and there it would seem Mary fixed her home, for every other mention of her during the ministry of the Lord is connected with Capernaum; and thither He, who henceforth had no home on earth, "had not where to lay His head," returned, after His journeys through the cities and villages teaching and healing—after the sermon on the mountain where the lilies grew and over which towered the highland fortress, "the city set on a hill, which could not be hid." There he sate on the shores, with the lake rippling at His feet, and taught; thence He crossed the waters in the fisher's boat ; in the synagogue there He spake as never man spake, calmly declaring that not His doctrine, but Himself, was the bread from heaven, and the life of the world ; there His brethren doubted and His disciples believed.

It may be that Mary went up with Him to the feast, and followed Him in His journeyings ; and that she as well as Johanna the wife of Chuza, Herod's steward, and the Magdalene and the other women from Galilee, ministered unto Him. But she could not have been young ; her life had not been one of luxury ; and in that Eastern climate old age succeeds to youth but with a brief twilight. Her name is not mentioned as among those who went up with Him on that last journey to Jerusalem, and as they followed were amazed and afraid. Yet we find her, when all had forsaken Him and fled, close by the cross, near enough to catch His dying accents. To the sepulchre, where Mary Magdalene and Mary the wife of Cleophas came early, Mary the mother of Jesus seems not to have come. It may be that the sword had pierced too deep into her heart, and that, true to her character, she pondered that last message in the home of the beloved disciple; it may be that a hope others could not see had dawned on the soul of her who had received Gabriel's glorious prophecy, and seen the shepherds and Magi worship Him in the manger, to whose faith the miracle of Cana was no surprise; and that Mary knew spices and ointments were not needed to embalm the body of that Holy One who could never see corruption.

But if the silence which wraps the childhood of Jesus has its lesson, the veil which hides from us the life of Mary during the years of our Lord's ministry, seems closed with too firm a purpose not to indicate a definite and prophetic meaning.

He who sees the full development of heresies before they spring, has not surely selected without purpose from those three years of her life precisely and only those incidents which prove that, as the mother of Jesus, she has no power with God. The only mention we have of her during those years are, when at Cana it is shown that the authority of the mortal mother, so long and dutifully submitted to, had ceased for ever; and when she, with his brethren, desired to speak with Him, He declared that for Him there was now another Family, bound to Him by stronger and more lasting ties than any which he had ever known at Nazareth.

I suppose most of us have felt something of a chill, in spite of all the explanations of commentators, at those words, " Woman, what have I to do with thee ?"—severing with so keen an edge the ties of years. It is difficult not to imagine they must have fallen bitterly on the mother's heart. Yet it does not seem that they did. It was another saying for Mary to ponder ; and her next words, the last we hear her speak, are full of an assured trust in His goodness and power.

Does not this undefined chill arise from the want of a fuller apprehension of the tenderness and sacredness of that eternal relationship which binds together the Church and the Lord ? Mary lost nothing by that transfer. Blessed as she was in being the mother of her Lord, she was rather blessed in being His disciple ; in being the handmaid of the Lord ; in knowing the will of God and doing it. It was a greater honour to be seated among that believing band who waited at Jerusalem for the promise of the Father, than to be obeyed by Jesus as the child in the old home at Nazareth.

Yet, essential and clear as this truth is, such

is the sacred tenderness of those natural affections wherewith God has bound us, that we could scarcely venture to apply it in this instance, had not our Lord Himself done so, with that "*rather* blessed"—"who is my mother and my brethren?" and even in that last, and most precious proof of affection, in the very dying testament to John on the cross from the lips parched with the thirst of agony—when He said to the beloved disciple, not "Behold *My* mother," but "Behold *thy* mother;" and to Mary, not "Mother," but "*Woman*, behold thy son."

To comprehend this, we need not to deaden natural affection, nor to slacken one earthly tie which binds us together, nor to sober down any glow of natural tenderness; but to quicken our spiritual affections, and to convert spiritual relationship into something very different from the cool affair of the judgment it too often is. We need to have written on our renewed hearts, in lines as deep and plain as the impulses of family affection, those words of Jesus, when He stretched forth His hands toward His disciples, and said, "*Behold my mother and my brethren.*" Renewed life has also its instincts. The new nature has also its natural affections : the family of God on earth should be so closely knit together, that the heart would bound with as instinctive an emotion towards a fellow Christian as towards a mother or a sister. It will be thus in heaven ; and in some faint degree, hindered by a thousand hindrances from within and without, is it not so even now on earth ?

The source of all spiritual kindred is in our relation to God as our Father in heaven, and to Him of whom the whole family in heaven and earth is named. So essentially is this the case, that when the spring of love to God is full, it must overflow in love to man; and if our love to the household of faith waxes cold, the surest way to warm it is not by poring over our cold-heartedness, and endeavouring to throw ourselves into a fervour of benevolence, but by *spending an hour alone with God*, reading of His love, telling Him of our lack of it— thinking of the love of Him who shrank not from the cross to save us, and in His purposes for our happiness is content with nothing but having His joy fulfilled in us—" As Thou, Father, art in Me, and I in Thee, that they may be one in us."

From that prayer, from that cross, pondering

these things (brought to our remembrance by the Comforter) in our hearts, with what a strong and grateful and humble affection should we go forth to the contest with daily annoyances, to the bearing of one another's burdens, to our daily task of forbearance, service, teaching, succouring. How near the redeemed of our Lord would be to our hearts! how inspiring their joys! how sacred their sorrows!

Relationship to God! union with Christ! The subject is not one for many words. But to the feeblest believer these are facts; to the weakest faith, which, looking at the depths of sin within, and then to Jesus crucified and risen, can scarcely do more than weep, and say, "*Lord, this seems too great to be true,*" proving its reality by its very doubting—this is an actual possession, though the joyful consciousness of it may not come until Jesus is seen "standing on the right hand of God," waiting to receive the departing spirit. God gives according to His measure, not according to ours; with His hand full—and in it, bound together by eternal love, and signed with the blood of His Son, are pardon, sanctification and glory.

"My *mother*, and *sister*, and *brother*." Not a word ever fell from His lips which was not laden with meaning. What, then, can these words mean, but that there is not a relationship on earth the tenderness of which His love does not contain and exceed, and the want of which He, in his own person, cannot fully supply? There is not a vacant place in the heart or the home He cannot fill, nor an energy of the renewed affections which may not find its full exercise through Him. Personally, Jesus can be, and designs to be this to those who believe in Him. In the abundance of natural ties, in the fullest home, and the life richest in natural influence and necessary activity, the heart of the Christian can find rest in none but Christ; and in the most solitary life, in the emptiest home, though it be but the one hired room, where domestic plans and labours lose all their poetry and sweetness by becoming merely the necessary providing for self, those meals which in the family are such happy gatherings and focuses of family history sinking into nothing more than the sustenance of the body—the love and the presence of Jesus can entirely satisfy the heart, and make it not only always content, but often in a glow of thankfulness, turning the solitary meal into a feast of gladness, and hallowing the solitary room with high and sweet associations. I believe not only that this is possible, but that it has been, and at this moment is, the case in many a home known but to God and the angels who minister there.

Yet though to faith the Lord himself is indeed present, He has left us, in sight, many a living representative, many a needy and harassed one included in that "Me." In this sense, the vicars of Christ on earth are many. How blessed might our lives be, if, from communion with Him in secret, we could go forth and recognize Him in every disciple we meet, and find Him in the cottage, in the school, in the home; from praying to Him in private, we could pass to ministering to Him in society—our social intercourse becoming thus almost as sacred as our prayers.

God is not only the God of all the families of the earth; He is the Father of the One Family in heaven and earth; and it is in the exercise of the affections of this eternal Family, and the ministries of this heavenly household, that our earthly homes are hallowed, and earthly bereavements soothed. We are members of a Family. We are not only not orphans, we have not only a Father in heaven—we have brothers and sisters on earth. We are taught to say, as we pray, not only "Father," but "*our* Father."

Have we not all felt the reality of this relationship, cementing new friendships as with the strength of years by the bond of common hope and common experience? Have we not felt it in the foreign city, giving to the unknown streets a look of familiarity, because we have discovered some of our kindred there? in the chance meeting with a stranger, when some unexpected word revealed the family-tie, and the varieties of early habit, national tastes, ecclesiastical associations, melted like the snow of a night in that living unity which the Holy Ghost alone can produce? when in a new neighbourhood we have met with the welcome of old friends for the love of Christ, and found ourselves suddenly as it were in the midst of a family circle?

But it is not in such occasional intercourse that the strength of the heavenly relationship is most tried. In the religious assembly, where we meet only as Christ's disciples, it is easy to look round and feel the heart warmed with the emotion of an ideal fraternity. It is not with strangers that this bond is least easily felt. It is when the petty subjects of daily intercourse distract us—when the little narrownesses, and infirmities, and rivalries, and caprices of others, rouse up our own stock of the same material, that we are in danger of losing sight of this most real and happy bond. In meeting one of whom we know but the one Hope held in common, only the Christian feeling is called forth; in meeting with the members of the same domestic circle, of the same congregation, of the same social class, of the same neighbourhood, or in consequence of the many other accidental ties which bind us—the higher relationship is in danger of being eclipsed by the nearer, the living union is in danger of being lost sight of in the nameless uncongeniality, the difference of natural character, or of conventional taste. All the harmony of the spheres may be entirely drowned in the discord of the street music or the fireside debate. It requires far more of the constraining love of Christ to love our cousins and neighbours as members of the heavenly family, than to feel the heart warm to our suffering brethren in Tuscany or Madeira. To love the whole Church, is one thing; to love—that is, to delight in the graces and veil the defects—of the person who misunderstood me and opposed my plans yesterday, whose peculiar infirmities grate on my most sensitive feelings, or whose natural faults are precisely those from which my natural character most revolts, is quite another: not only because platform enthusiasm and home affection have altogether a different measure of reality, but because in the one case only what is Christian is appealed to, and in the other Christian love has to contend with a legion of dwarfish foes, whose million pin-pricks hurt and irritate more than one giant blow, no one thinking it necessary to apply to the Physician for injuries so trifling.

But this need not be so. The daily intercourse of life might deepen our spiritual communion instead of superseding it. The natural tie might strengthen the spiritual. That reserve which so often walls up the heart from those nearest us, may yield to a confidence which, once attained, no communion on earth can equal. Mutual infirmities, necessarily known to one another, and together confessed to the Father in heaven, may unite us more closely than common success and joy. If we could only learn, whilst dealing with our own infirmities as sins, to regard the faults of those dear to us as we would their afflictions, being as tender and as prayerful over their spiritual as we would over their bodily sickness; or, better still, if we could look on one another's faults as *common* enemies—blending with our every-day occupations and pleasures the light of heavenly hopes and the energy of heavenly aims—praying together as those only can, the inmost secrets and homeliest details of whose lives are known to one another—our homes might indeed become sanctuaries, our families the two or three gathered together in Christ's name, where He is in the midst; our social intercourse as hallowed as our religious assemblies. The eternal and most real kindred of the children of God would give intensity to the natural relationship; the double bond would form a chain whose elastic strength nothing could break; and when the perishable tie must be severed, the eternal would still unite us with a hope as dear as the memory of what we had lost, and under the dress of mourning, the heart would wear the garments of hope.

But to keep this heavenly relationship real and fresh, we need, avove all, love to the Saviour; then deep consciousness of what we are, what we have been forgiven, from what we have been saved, and, lastly, that the heart should be kept unspotted from the world. Love to God, an humble because truthful opinion of ourselves, and unworldliness—this is the threefold cord of spiritual affection.

Even in earthly relationships, before the eager chases of ambition, and in the cool atmosphere of conventional intercourse, the memories of the old home dissolve into very remote and bloodless shades. The world would persuade us that its artificial flowers are the true. Do not the others fade and fall? and what is their fragrance but a mere intangible breath? But with the spiritual kindred this is still more the case. We cannot choose our companions for some adventitious congeniality, similarity of taste, cultivation, position, without finding the reality of that eternal kindred fade into a very cool and distant connection—" brethren" declining itself into a very different singular from "brother," until, at last, we only realize the bond on Sundays when we say the Apostles' Creed, and then place the "communion of saints" in very much the same era as the "resurrection of the body." It is not as liking the same books, having the same religious tastes, agreeing in the minute distinctions of Scriptural interpretation, that our Lord would have us united; but as having the same Father, and being called by the same Name. Opinion can merely bind together, it cannot fuse into one; its attraction is mechanical, not chemical—adhesion instead of combination. Knowledge, uninspired by love, is an ever-narrowing basis of union. It is not liking the same doctrines, but loving the same Saviour, that truly unites us. The tie we are bound by is not one of congeniality, but one of kindred, as real and as innate in the child of God, as the love of a father or mother, a brother, or sister, or child. The relationship exists; the family is around us; let us not forget the responsibility, and thus miss the joy.

For although heaven may not recognize the family ties, or re-knit, as such, the family groups of earth, those groups need not be scattered, nor those ties slackened. It will be One Home and One Family, and each among the blessed there will surely love each with a love tenderer and stronger than the tenderest and purest affection we can know here. We shall not be further from our beloved, but nearer to them. If from the thought of the breaking up of the families of earth, as from the words, "Woman, what have I to do with thee?" the heart shrinks at times with an undefined dread, is it not simply because we do not feel the blessed reality and power of those other words, "Behold my mother and my brethren?" The memories of earth's hallowed intercourse and affection cannot perish in the presence of Him who loved Mary and her sister, and Lazarus. We may be quite sure that every yearning of the heart will be fully satisfied, and every energy of the affections employed to its full intensity in that day when Mary and "the beloved disciple," and the "brethren of the Lord," shall be gathered with the whole family in the Father's house, and the Church, the ransomed Bride, shall enter into the joy of her Lord.

"SHE IS NOT DEAD, BUT SLEEPETH."

1 Corinthians xv. 6.

Some are fallen asleep.

VII.

"SHE IS NOT DEAD, BUT SLEEPETH."

HE last society we find Mary in is among the disciples: the last employment we see her engaged in is prayer.
We know that the home of the disciple whom Jesus loved was hers; and we know that, years afterwards, St. Paul found St. John at Jerusalem. We know that the intercourse between her who could tell of the home of the "child Jesus" of Nazareth, and him who had listened to the promise of the many mansions in the Father's house—between her who had watched over the infancy of the Lord, and him who had leaned on His breast, must have had a tenderness and a sacredness, a reverence and intimacy, scarcely again to be found on earth. But how long this lasted we do not know, nor how it closed.

The Bible gives us very few death-bed

scenes. The New Testament describes but two deaths—the Crucifixion and the stoning of the first martyr. "Father, forgive them, for they know not what they do," and "Father, into Thy hands I commend my spirit;" "Lord Jesus receive my spirit," and "Lord, lay not this sin to their charge," are the only dying words the New Testament records.

Silently all those early believers pass to their rest. Mary Magdalene, and Mary and Martha, and Lazarus, "who had been dead, whom Jesus raised from the dead;" John the beloved, Paul the aged, Peter, and Mary the mother of Jesus, not a sign indicates to us how they died.

We only know that they believed and loved, laboured and suffered, and fought a good fight, and that now they rest and rejoice. That unnatural severing of body and spirit which sin brought into the world, which one generation of the Church, like Enoch, shall escape, not sleeping, but being changed, is passed over in silence: it seems as if we were meant to think of their life in heaven as but a calm continuation of their life on earth, without its hindrances or its pains.

"Ever with the Lord," in that state which is far happier and holier, and better, than the life of the most devoted apostle on earth, they yet wait to be "clothed upon with the house which is from heaven."

The mysteries of that intermediate world we cannot penetrate, near as it may be; we only know, if the parable of Lazarus may be taken as a revelation, as well as an exhortation, that there is communion there with one another as well as with the Lord; that Lazarus leans on Abraham's breast, as at the Last Supper the beloved disciple leaned on the breast of Jesus. Those dear ones who have entered there, may have held communion, ere this, with her whose history we can here trace only in such broken glimpses, as with the saints of the older dispensation.

Of Mary we are sure that, not as the mortal mother, still less as the widowed and the aged, does she abide in the resting-place and wait the Trump of the Archangel; but as one young with the youth of angels, one whose every tear has been wiped away, one who, with all who have fallen asleep in Jesus, abides in perpetual communion with Him.

And when He shall come again with clouds, and every eye shall see Him, amongst the ten thousands of His saints who shall come with

Him, when what is "sown in weakness shall be raised in power"—amongst the multitude, which no man can number, of His redeemed—will be Mary the handmaid of the Lord, blessed in having been the mother of the Lord, but how far rather blessed in being the child of God and the disciple of Jesus—in being able to sing with the whole ransomed family for ever :

"My soul doth magnify the Lord, and my spirit hath rejoiced in God my Saviour!"

www.ingramcontent.com/pod-product-compliance
Lightning Source LLC
Chambersburg PA
CBHW030339170426
43202CB00010B/1180